The Wallace Effect

The Wallace Effect

David Foster Wallace and the Contemporary Literary Imagination

Marshall Boswell

BLOOMSBURY ACADEMIC
NEW YORK • LONDON • OXFORD • NEW DELHI • SYDNEY

BLOOMSBURY ACADEMIC
Bloomsbury Publishing Inc
1385 Broadway, New York, NY 10018, USA
50 Bedford Square, London, WC1B 3DP, UK

First published in the United States of America 2019

Cover design: Daniel Benneworth-Gray
Cover image © Creative Commons

A catalog record for this book is available from the Library of Congress.

ISBN: HB: 978-1-5013-4494-7
PB: 978-1-5013-4490-9
ePDF: 978-1-5013-4492-3
eBook: 978-1-5013-4491-6

Series: David Foster Wallace Studies

Typeset by Newgen KnowledgeWorks Pvt. Ltd., Chennai, India
Printed and bound in the United States of America

To find out more about our authors and books, visit www.bloomsbury.com
and sign up for our newsletters.

for Rebecca

CONTENTS

SERIES EDITOR'S INTRODUCTION

The first volume in this series—Lucas Thompson's *Global Wallace*—offered an intensive study of Wallace's works, picking apart the texture of his intricately crafted oeuvre to reveal their often overlooked borrowings from, and allusions to, the corpus of world literature. The second volume in this series—which you are now holding in your hands—reverses this approach and, instead of tracing the recurrence of other works and writers within Wallace's texts, maps the place of his fiction in the wider field of contemporary American literature. Yet, despite their different angles of approach, both studies seek to enlarge our map of the literary world within which Wallace wrote. If Thompson's volume provided a timely corrective to the provincial impulse to confine a reading within American borders, then Marshall Boswell's study challenges the widespread tendency for Wallace studies to treat Wallace's work as *sui generis* within those borders, by deepening our sense of the context out of which Wallace wrote, and by measuring the sometimes ambivalent impact Wallace had on other writers, which Boswell calls the "Wallace Effect."

The fact of Wallace's influence on contemporary literature is, by now, well established and widely noted. Jeffrey Severs, for instance, begins his excellent study of value in Wallace's work by arguing that his fiction "signalled a sharp turn against postmodernist tenets" and galvanized a "new phase in contemporary global literature" (1). Yet what is often overlooked is the extent to which that influence has overspilled the boundaries of any particular *type* of fiction. The experimental edge of his output, and his early sympathies for "extreme avant-garde shit" (*Conversations* 71), help account for his appeal to innovative writers at independent presses whose work abandons the codes and comforts of the well-made realist novel. Bennett Sims, for instance, dedicates his virtuosic reformulation of the zombie novel, *A Questionable Shape* (2013), to Wallace and bends his signature footnotes to match the book's content ("the footnote digs a grave in the text, an underworld in the text" [16n1]). Similarly, Evan Lavender-Smith's *From Old Notebooks* (2010) adopts the style of David Markson's late works and periodically punctuates its atomistic structure with ideas about and reflections upon Wallace's fiction:

> Essay describing the structure of *Infinite Jest* as Hofstadterish *strange loop*, the novel's structure being that of a circle with a missing section. (15)
>
> David Foster Wallace is at his very best when he transforms the temperature of a particular mode of language from cold to warm. (114)

At the same time, it is equally common to find Wallace namechecked in more mainstream works. Thus, in Paul Beatty's prizewinning *The Sellout* (2015), Foy Cheshire casually announces that his "reimagined multicultural text, *Of Rice and Yen*," will put him in the company of "Virginia Woolf, Kawabata, Mishima, Mayakovsky, and DFW" (253).

Such references do not, of course, automatically indicate a uniformly detailed engagement with Wallace's legacy and—in some instances—more accurately reflect the way Wallace's name has become a floating signifier for variously amorphous cultural yearnings. Beatty's namecheck is notable in this respect, inasmuch as he uses the quasi-brand name "DFW" rather than anything more personal and submerges his name in a list whose unity comes not from any shared style but from these writers' fame as suffering artists. While it is no doubt significant that Beatty's list reaches beyond the common canon of white tortured artists—Kawabata rather than Plath; Mishima rather than Hemingway—and while *The Sellout*'s book-length meditation on what happens to individual identity when everything about identity is subjected to relentless satire is not entirely divorced from Wallace's own concerns, two salient points emerge from such examples. The first is that the mere invocation of a name offers insufficient grounds for documenting the extent of Wallace's relevance to a text; the second is that Wallace's biography mingles with his literary achievements as contemporary fictions come to terms with his legacy. Marshall Boswell's *The Wallace Effect* is the first full-length study of Wallace's impact on American letters, and it is decisively attuned to such complexities that emerge from his legacy. In terms of the breadth of Wallace's influence, the book offers the fullest studies to date of two of the key figures—Jonathan Franzen and Jeffrey Eugenides—who are most often associated with Wallace in that "sharp turn against postmodernist tenets." But it also looks beyond those writers who were sufficiently indebted to postmodernism for a turn to be necessary, by addressing Wallace's place in Claire Messud's realist fiction, and—in a chapter partly devoted to Lauren Groff—challenging the male-centric model of literary achievement that is regularly invoked to measure Wallace's work. In addressing this cast of authors, Boswell's study zeroes in on the question of when and where Wallace's influence can reasonably be attributed and is especially alert to those instances where an author explicitly denies Wallace's "ghostly appearance" in their text. Across the whole book, these studies come together to document the way that these spectral appearances construct "Wallace" as a composite figure, partly assembled from the signature obsessions that run through his texts, but also drawing freely on his biography.

Boswell's readings are eclectic and typically comprehensive, but they also open the door for readers to move outside his shortlist of novels and pursue further iterations of the Wallace Effect. After reading Boswell's detailed account of the way Franzen diffuses Wallace trademarks throughout *Freedom*, the significance of Franzen's persistent, yet apparently more subdued, allusions in *Purity* (2015) merit further attention: in a book rife with allusions to *Hamlet*, Tom Aberant almost echoes Wallace's assignment to follow John McCain for *Rolling Stone* when he passes "up an opportunity to follow the Dukakis campaign for *Rolling Stone*" (409), while Anabel reprises one of the movies from James Incandenza's filmography in *Infinite Jest* ("*Every Inch of Disney Leith*" [989n24]) via her plan to divide her body into "a grid of 32-square-centimeter 'cuts'" that will each be individually filmed (401). Similarly, in light of Boswell's exploration of how "the Wallace Effect registers an unmistakable strain of sexual menace," the fact that Jennifer Egan's parody of Wallace's style in *A Visit from the Goon Squad* is also an explicit study of sexual menace may merit further examination.

SERIES EDITOR'S INTRODUCTION

Yet as *The Wallace Effect* points forward to later novels, it also—crucially—directs its gaze sideways and backward. In much Wallace criticism, "postmodernist tenets" are confined to an imaginary past, where they are archived as historical, immutable facts. Following Wallace's own cues, John Barth, in particular, is forever locked in 1968 and denied the considerable artistic development that followed his landmark, yet arguably not-especially representative, achievements in *Lost in the Funhouse*. That this tendency has perpetuated misreadings of Wallace's place in literary history has gradually been addressed by essays such as Charles B. Harris's "The Anxiety of Influence" (2014) and Mary K. Holland's "Your Head Gets in the Way" (2016), which substantially nuance and qualify what Wallace learnt from Barth's funhouse. But Boswell's particular achievement in the first part of this book is to draw our attention to the fact that not only did Barth—and postmodernism itself—exist in fluid progress through the decades when Wallace was articulating his critique of both but also that Barth was himself undertaking a continual process of self-criticism and creative revision. That the border lines between literary generations are not as limpid as many conventional accounts suggest is reinforced by Boswell's chapter on Richard Powers. While we might think of Powers as having written his own Wallace Effect novel in *Generosity* (2009), Boswell's account reveals how in significant, and largely unheralded, ways, Powers preceded his contemporary in exploring many of the same concerns that dogged Wallace through the late 1980s and early 1990s. *The Wallace Effect*, then, is on one level a study of a single writer's impact, but it is also a study that encourages us to think of literary history as a mobile configuration of parallel developments, rather than as a static, linear sequence of fixed monuments.

The need to rethink Wallace's place in literary history in this way reflects the arc of Wallace scholarship across the last two decades. The intricate architecture and flamboyant stylistic virtuosity of Wallace's fiction required the first phase of Wallace scholarship to focus on literary aesthetics: to explain the purpose of apparent stylistic excesses, to untangle the scrambled chronology of *Infinite Jest*, and to identify hidden patterns where detractors saw formless chaos. With much of that work done, an increasingly vital task for recent Wallace criticism has been to situate his fiction and ask questions about its place in larger contexts: how, for example, questions of race (Tara Morrissey and Lucas Thompson, Samuel

Cohen, Edward Jackson and Joel Roberts) and gender (Clare Hayes-Brady, Mary K. Holland) complicate Wallace's position; how place—especially the Midwest and its regional narratives—filters into his writing (Jurrit Daalder); and how his treatment of therapy and depression relate to longer traditions (Jamie Redgate). *The Wallace Effect*, in many ways, is part of this movement, but as it adds substantial detail to our sense of Wallace's literary context, it also "completes" a substantial phase of Marshall Boswell's work. With *Understanding David Foster Wallace* (2003)—surely by some distance the most cited piece of Wallace scholarship—and his later essays on *Oblivion* ("The Constant Monologue inside Your Head") and *The Pale King* ("Trickle-Down Citizenship" and "Author Here"), Boswell has written detailed analyses of every book of fiction Wallace published. With *The Wallace Effect*, he has produced a vital companion study to those studies, turning his attention from the intricacies of the Wallace text to the complex questions raised by his context.

Stephen J. Burn

Works Cited

Beatty, Paul. *The Sellout*. London: Oneworld, 2015.

Franzen, Jonathan. *Purity*. New York: Farrar, 2015.

Harris, Charles B. "The Anxiety of Influence: The John Barth/David Foster Wallace Connection." *Critique 55*, no. 2 (2014): 103–26.

Holland, Mary K. "'Your Head Gets in the Way': Reflecting (on) Realism from Barth to Wallace." *John Barth: A Body of Words*. Ed. Gabrielle Dean and Charles B. Harris. Victoria, TX: Dalkey, 2016. 201–31.

Lavender-Smith, Evan. *From Old Notebooks*. Buffalo, NY: BlazeVOX, 2010.

Severs, Jeffrey. *David Foster Wallace's Balancing Books: Fictions of Value*. New York: Columbia, 2017.

Sims, Bennett. *A Questionable Shape*. N.p.: Two Dollar Radio, 2013.

Wallace, David Foster. *Conversations with David Foster Wallace*. Ed. Stephen J. Burn. Jackson: UP of Mississippi, 2012.

Introduction

"Next year's book awards have been decided," declared Walter Kirn in his February 1996 review of David Foster Wallace's postmodern meganovel, *Infinite Jest*. "The plaques and citations can now be put in escrow. With *Infinite Jest* . . . —a plutonium-dense, satirical quiz-kid opus that runs to almost a thousand pages (not including footnotes)—the competition has been obliterated" (Kirn 54). Although *Infinite Jest* would in fact *not* win a single major award in the year following its publication, this oversight on the part of the nation's literary gatekeepers hardly halted the novel's irresistible momentum. As David Lipsky recalls in his Wallace memoir, *Infinite Jest*'s initial impact on the contemporary literary landscape had the seismic effect of an asteroid strike. At a New York party that same February, a female acquaintance of Lipsky's told him, "Every anxious writer I know is obsessed with [Wallace], because he did what they wanted to do" (Lipsky xxv). She also revealed that "all these relationships are being screwed up by David Foster Wallace. All these men—because they secretly want to *be* David Foster Wallace—they flip out whenever he's in the paper. All the girls are like 'David Foster Wallace, he's really cool.' So the guys are like, 'I *hate* David Foster Wallace'" (xxiv–xxv).

What I am calling the Wallace Effect refers to the mixture of envy, hagiography, and resentment that has come to mark Wallace's presence in the contemporary literary imagination. Kirn's declaration that, with *Infinite Jest*, "the competition has been obliterated" captures this dynamic but so does Lipsky's account of the "anxious" writers who both coveted Wallace's achievement and

hated him for it. In the years following his 2008 suicide, he has been
lionized as a postmodern saint in some quarters and vilified as a
pretentious, misogynist "lit-bro" in others. That same, contradictory
blend of hero worship and score-settling also characterizes his
presence in the work of his contemporaries. It is remarkable enough
that Wallace, who was born in 1962, has already been the subject
of a major motion picture, the sort of treatment usually reserved
for ex-presidents, dead music legends, sports heroes, or Ernest
Hemingway. But he has also made ghostly appearances in several
major novels of the last two decades, wherein fictional characters
don his trademark bandana, affect his speaking style, and/or suffer
from his addiction to Skoal dipping snuff. These characters also
often share his depression, his substance addiction, and his sexual
promiscuity. The novels both confirm Wallace's broad influence on
the contemporary literary sensibility and push back against the
monolithic centrality of his position as contemporary US literature's
uncontested top dog.

If David Foster Wallace is in fact recognized—however
grudgingly—as the most important and influential writer of his
generation, this is largely because Wallace set out deliberately to
earn that status. His early work leading up to *Infinite Jest*, the book
that established and continues to sustain his stature, makes no
secret of its author's vaunting ambition. That body of work also
frames his bid for literary greatness in stark and uncompromisingly
competitive terms. For Wallace, who once described himself as a
"near great tennis junior player," writing fiction was a struggle for
supremacy (*Supposedly* 3). In both his fiction and his nonfiction
from the late 1980s and early 1990s, he listed or alluded to the
literary forebears with whom he wished to be associated and whom
he sought to vanquish. He also insistently identified himself as
part of a new generation of writers possessed of an urgent new
sensibility—one most successfully exemplified by his own work.
If you were a member of the old guard, Wallace had put you on
notice. If you were his contemporary, you now occupied a satellite
position in the new movement he was willing into existence. With
Infinite Jest, he amply fulfilled all the audacious claims he had made
for himself.

His first two works of fiction established his battle plan for
artistic ascendency. *The Broom of the System*, his auspicious 1987
debut, owes a deep debt to Thomas Pynchon's *The Crying of Lot*

49, about which Wallace was both touchy and defensive, so much so that in 1996 he complained, "It was hard when that book came out because the Japanese lady from *The New York Times* and other people said it was a rip-off of *The Crying of Lot 49*, which in my own defense I claim I had not read at that time" ("Lost 1996 Interview").[1] Strictly speaking, this claim is untrue. According to Mark Costello, Wallace's college roommate at Amherst, Wallace first encountered *The Crying of Lot 49* during his sophomore year, an experience that was "like Bob Dylan finding Woody Guthrie"; another of Wallace's college friends dismissed the novel as "a Pynchon rip-off" (Max 31, 48). The connections are certainly hard to ignore. The novel's bewildered female heroine, Lenore Beadsman, clearly invokes Pynchon's Oedipa Mass, while her crackpot therapist, Dr. Jay, bears more than a passing resemblance to Pynchon's LSD-addled Dr. Hilarius. And the early description of East Corinth, Ohio, the novel's principle setting, as resembling "a profile of Jayne Mansfield" recalls Oedipa Mass's hilltop comparison of *Lot 49*'s San Narciso with a "printed circuit" (*Broom* 45, *Lot 49* 24).[2] But Pynchon isn't the only influence, as the novel's stretches of dialogue absent tags and scenic description recall the work of William Gaddis, another major figure from the pantheon of US postmodern fiction writers. In a less talented and ambitious writer, such borrowings might signal a limited imagination; in the case of David Foster Wallace, his disingenuous denials notwithstanding, the allusions mark a pattern of artistic affinity. Wallace was firmly aligning himself with the tradition he hoped to join.

His single-minded ambition to ally himself with the tradition represented by Pynchon and Gaddis put him at odds with his workshop instructors at the University of Arizona (UA), where he pursued an masters of fine arts in fiction following his graduation

---

[1]The "Japanese lady" is Michiko Kakutani, who reviewed *The Broom of the System* in the *New York Times*. In that review, she argued, "From its opening pages onward through its enigmatic ending, *The Broom of the System* will remind readers of *The Crying of Lot 49* by Thomas Pynchon" (Kakutani 14).

[2]For a more thorough assessment of how Wallace both alludes to and updates Pynchon's novel, see *Understanding David Foster Wallace* (21–64). In an endnote, published a full decade before Max disproved the claim, I report Wallace's insistence that he read *The Crying of Lot 49* only *after* he published *The Broom of the System*, merely adding, "Though this is certainly possible, it seems somehow unlikely" (215).

from Amherst. Jonathan Penner, one of those instructors, regarded Wallace's flamboyant, sprawling metafiction a misuse of his talent, telling him at one point that "if he continued to write the way he was writing, '[Penner] would hate to lose him'" (Max 64). Wallace was having none of it. The stories he wrote at UA, later collected in *Girl with Curious Hair*, continued his program of name-checking and score-settling. The title story, narrated by a catatonic yuppie sociopath with a predilection for sexual violence, devastatingly parodies the work of Bret Easton Ellis, anticipating by two years Ellis's own scabrous novel of sociopathic yuppie violence, *American Psycho*, which appeared in 1991. "Lyndon," which features the thirty-sixth US president and his first lady as fictional characters, tips its cap to Robert Coover's *The Public Burning*, while the hillbilly cadences of "John Billy" point back to *Omensetter's Luck* by William Gass. As Max observes, in this latter tussle with one of his postmodern precursors, Wallace introduces "an element of parody in the homage. The goal was to push the original out of sight" (74).[3] In the collection's final piece, "Westward the Course of Empire Takes its Way," addressed at greater length in Chapter 1, Wallace takes aim at his own workshop instructors via a complex critique of traditional metafiction that directly targets the work of John Barth while also digressing into essayistic dismissals of the truck-stop minimalism favored by his Arizona professors and perfected by Raymond Carver and Gordon Lish, the latter of whom Wallace calls out by name (265).

Bret Easton Ellis was not the only contemporary writer Wallace identified as a threatening rival. In a series of essays and interviews he published in the years prior to *Infinite Jest*, he took on his young competitors one by one. In "Fictional Futures and the Conspicuously Young," he effectively dismissed most of his "C.Y."

---

[3]Wallace would pay homage to Gass once again in 1992, at the conclusion of his review of H. L. Hix's *Morte D'Author: An Autopsy*, which traces the scholarly impact of Roland Barthes' "Death of the Author" essay. Significantly, Wallace basically gives Gass, whom he defines as a member of the "anti-death" camp, the essay's final word, suggesting that, in this case, the master speaks for the student. Paraphrasing from Gass's *Habitations of the Word*, Wallace argues that "critics can try to erase or over-define the author into anonymity for all sorts of technical, political, and philosophical reasons, and"—quoting Gass directly now—"'this 'anonymity' may mean many things, but one thing which it cannot mean is that no one did it'" (*Supposedly* 145; *Habitations* 273).

contemporaries—a list that includes Ellis, Jay McInerney, Tama Janovitz, David Leavitt, Mona Simpson, and Susan Minot—as products of media hype. In levying this assessment, he also took one last swipe at his precursors. "It's true enough that some cringingly bad fiction gets written by C.Y.'s," he declared. "But that is hardly an explanation for anything, since the same is true of lots of older artists, many of whom have clearly shot their bolts and now hang by name and fashion alone" (*Both Flesh* 39). Not accidentally, that last sentence contains a quotation from John Barth's 1967 essay "The Literature of Exhaustion," in which Barth gives credence to those writers of his time who felt "that the novel, if not narrative literature generally, if not the printed word altogether, has by this hour of the world shot its bolt" (*The Friday Book* 71). Five years later, in "E Unibus Pluram," he took on the so-called Image Fiction of Mark Leyner and found it not up to the task of assuaging the solipsism and cynicism of his own generation of "sad kids." Leyner's work and others like it is "hilarious, upsetting, sophisticated, and extremely shallow—doomed to shallowness by its desire to ridicule a TV-culture whose mockery itself and all value already absorbs ridicule" (*Supposedly* 81). Finally, in his now fetishized 1993 interview with Larry McCaffery, he took particular aim once again at Ellis, who, in the wake of the scandal surrounding *American Psycho*, was the most famous, or infamous, writer of Wallace's generation at that time. Ellis's work, Wallace argues, essentially suffers from the imitative fallacy. As he explains, "If what's always distinguished bad writing—flat characters, a narrative world that's clichéd and not recognizably human, etc.—is also a description of today's world, then bad writing becomes an ingenious mimesis of a bad world"; *American Psycho*, by extension, is "a mean shallow stupid novel that becomes a mordant deadpan commentary on the badness of everything" (*Conversations* 26).[4] Conversely, Wallace insists that the definition of "good art would seem to be art that locates and applies CPR to those elements of what's human that still live and glow despite the times' darkness" (26).

---

[4]Wallace's battle with Ellis continues into *Infinite Jest*. A key character from the novel, Joelle van Dyne, hosts a popular radio show under the pseudonym Madame Psychosis in which she reads aloud from a range of texts and sources. For a period she refers to her program as "Madame's Downer-Lit Hour," which featured what the narrator calls "a truly ghastly Bret Ellis period during Lent" (191).

As has by now become nearly axiomatic in Wallace scholarship, "E Unibus Pluram" can be read as Wallace's most direct rallying cry for a new literary sensibility. While ostensibly analyzing the complex ways in which 1990s "TV-culture" has appropriated postmodern irony, the essay lays out possible avenues contemporary writers might explore going forward to move beyond postmodern irony and toward a more engaged and earnest fiction. As such, the essay provides a much more direct articulation of various ideas hinted at in the pages of "Westward" and other stories from the *Girl with Curious Hair* collection such as "My Appearance" and "Little Expressionless Animals." Scholars have struggled to give this sensibility a suitable name; it has been called the post-postmodern, the post-ironic, or the New Sincerity. As so much work on this subject has already been done, I do not wish to rehearse these arguments here. For the purposes of this volume, I will simply reaffirm my own early explanation for Wallace's proposed new approach as a joining of cynicism and naiveté. These terms are Wallace's, and, as I have shown elsewhere, and will take up again in these pages, he uses these terms three times in straight succession, in the same basic formulation, in three key texts from the period under examination here. In "Westward," he identifies one character's solipsistic "delusion . . . that cynicism and naiveté are mutually exclusive" (304). He quotes himself again later in "E Unibus Pluram" when he asks, "Culture-wise, shall I spend much of your time pointing out the degree to which televisual values influence the contemporary mood of jaded weltschmerz, self-mocking materialism, blank indifference, and the delusion that cynicism and naiveté are mutually exclusive?" (*Supposedly* 63). Quoting himself yet again, he has his hero Hal Incandenza, deep in the depths of *Infinite Jest*, wonder about "that queerly persistent U.S. myth that cynicism and naiveté are mutually exclusive" (694). In all three instances, Wallace reveals his meaning negatively; turned around, these passages all insist that cynicism and naiveté are *not* mutually exclusive, and that it is a "delusion" to think so. For Wallace, "cynicism" encompasses a wide range of "hollowing out" strategies, from ironic distancing to metafictional self-consciousness, while "naiveté" embraces such shopworn notions as sentimentality, earnestness, and sincerity. Wallace's work embraces both in an unresolved dialectic that accounts for his fiction's sophisticated self-reflexivity and its heartfelt openness to what he calls at the end of "E Unibus Pluram" "single-entendre principles" (81).

"E Unibus Pluram" and the McCaffery interview would go on to have the impact Wallace intended for "Westward." The two pieces provided a much more lucid and inspiring description of the kind of art he hoped would succeed both seventies metafiction and eighties minimalism. They also considerably raised the stakes for Wallace's proposed conquest of the literary landscape, as they appeared side-by-side in an issue of *The Review of Contemporary Fiction* devoted exclusively to the work of Wallace, William Vollmann, and Susan Daitch. That same issue included a reminiscence of Wallace—who was all of thirty-one at the time—by the aforementioned Costello, two scholarly essays on Wallace's work by Lance Olsen and James Rother, respectively, and, most importantly, an excerpt from his forthcoming work, *Infinite Jest*, which Wallace had not completed at the time.[5] For those readers who were charmed by his first novel, *The Broom of the System*, and intrigued by the innovative, television-soaked stories in *Girl with Curious Hair*, the issue of *The Review of Contemporary Literature* whetted an appetite for the next thing to come. For aspiring writers of Wallace's own generation, this early scholarly attention must have left a very sore spot indeed.

Wallace continued to lay the groundwork for his conquest via the pages of *Harper's* magazine, where he published a series of personal essays that would greatly expand his readership. "Tennis, Trigonometry, and Tornadoes" (later retitled "Derivative Sport in Tornado Alley") appeared in 1992, "Ticket to the Fair" (later retitled "Getting Away from Already Being Pretty Much Away from It All") appeared in 1994, and "Shipping Out" (i.e., "A Supposedly Fun Thing I'll Never Do Again") appeared in January 1996, a month before *Infinite Jest*'s February publication. The latter piece appeared as a matte-paper insert in the magazine, without any ads to interrupt the reader's experience. Lipsky argues that the essay "cleared the landscape, cut the runway for his novel. People photocopied it, faxed it, read it aloud over the phone. He'd done a thing that was casual and gigantic; he'd captured everybody's brain voice" (xxviii). A month later, as Lipsky puts it, Wallace "earthquaked the city" (xxviii). At his standing-room-only readings in New York,

---

[5]The excerpt appears on pages 503–7 of the published novel.

celebrities such as Ethan Hawke showed up, clutching their fresh blue copies of Wallace's behemoth, while elsewhere, "women in the front rows batted their eyelashes, [and] men at the back huffed, scowled, envied" (xxix).

Lipsky's account of the Wallace earthquake touches a series of notes that have remained constant throughout his reception and which characterize the Wallace Effect as I outline it in the pages that follow, namely that Wallace's conquest was both literary and, in some way, sexual. The men in Lipsky's account don't just envy and resent Wallace's literary prowess, they also perceive him, accurately or not, as a sexual threat. If Lipsky's party attendee is to be believed, whole relationships fell apart solely because David Foster Wallace was profiled in the pages of the *New York Times Magazine*. A similar dynamic plays out strikingly in three of the novels addressed here. In each text, the fictional character in the novel who accesses something of Wallace's persona is presented as not only an intellectual and/or artistic genius but also a figure of tremendous, even dangerous, sexual potency. What's more, all three novels stage their very Wallace-esque games of artistic/intellectual competition in erotic terms. From its very inception to its current manifestation, the Wallace Effect registers an unmistakable strain of sexual menace.

Infinite Jest solidified Wallace's right to stand shoulder to shoulder with the precursors whose work he had invoked in his earlier fiction. Although the novel is as indebted to Pynchon's *Gravity's Rainbow* as *Broom* was to *Lot 49*, here the linkage is overt and confident. The shaded circles that signal chapter breaks in *Infinite Jest*, which suggest pharmaceutical pills and/or meniscus lenses, recall the series of squares—possibly suggesting spokes in a roll of celluloid film—that divide the discrete sections of *Gravity's Rainbow* and which were reduced to a single square for the Bantam trade paperback edition, likely the edition Wallace read. What's more, the novel's mix of cartoonish humor, dense scientific data, and encyclopedic sprawl match Pynchon's achievement point-by-point. Even the pervasive present-tense mode declares its debt. But *Infinite Jest* makes no attempt to hide its homage.[6] The creator of

---

[6]*Infinite Jest* also boasts one of Wallace's most direct allusions to *Gravity's Rainbow*. In the first of several episodes featuring Remy Maratha and Hugh Steeply in conversation atop a mountain in Tuscon, Arizona, Wallace describes Marathe

the novel's anchoring McGuffin, namely, the lethally entertaining film "Infinite Jest," is James Incandenza, the father of the novel's teenage hero, Hal Incandenza, a "near great junior tennis player" and lexical prodigy who clearly invokes his creator. Incandenza's filmography, which occupies a nine-page endnote, has widely been interpreted, by myself and others, as an "extended parody of the postmodern canon" (*Understanding* 162), while the novel's critique of Jim's artistic sensibility echoes Wallace's own critiques of the work of his postmodern fathers. In an oft-quoted passage, one of the novel's characters, and the star of the eponymously titled Entertainment, describes Incandenza's work as "technically gorgeous, . . . with lighting and angles planned out to the frame. But oddly hollow, empty, no sense of dramatic *towardness*—no narrative movement toward a real story; no emotional movement toward an audience" (740). As will be fleshed out in more detail in the pages that follow, this critique applies also to Wallace's view of the sort of postmodern metafiction that his work both invokes and seeks to overcome. It's all cynicism with no naiveté. His agenda with *Infinite Jest* is clear: he is seeking to match Pynchon at his own game and improve upon the master.

In the immediate wake of *Infinite Jest*'s triumph, a new breed of emergent writers began to borrow from Wallace and embrace the new sensibility he ushered into full fruition with his crowning work. Dave Eggers's free-wheeling, hyper-self-conscious, and doggedly earnest memoir *A Heartbreaking Work of Staggering Genius* was perhaps the first major work to borrow directly from Wallace's wheelhouse of tics and literary devices. (Wallace also blurbed the book.) The Wallace strain was also vividly apparent in the early work of writers such as Jonathan Safron Foer (*Everything*

"amusing himself" with his shadow, which is "enlarged and distended . . . far out overland," a distension the narrator likens to "Goethe's well known '*Brökengespenst*' phenomenon," which Wallace's narrator defines in a footnote as "Ghostly light- and monster-shadow phenomenon particular to certain mountains" (88, 994, n38). Wallace alludes here to a scene in *Gravity's Rainbow* in which Tyrone Slothrop, the novel's schleppy anti-hero, and his temporary lover Geli Tripping stand atop Broken Mountain in Germany and cast "two gigantic shadows, thrown miles overland" (330). The narrator explains that the resulting "Specter" is known in the area as "the Brokengespenst," minus the umlaut (330). The full German name for the phenomenon Wallace has in mind is the Brockengespenstphänomen (331), which might be where he found his misplaced umlaut.

Is Illuminated, Extremely Loud and Extremely Close), Benjamin Kunkel (*Indecision*), and Mark Danielewski (*House of Leaves*), just to name a few. All of these works combined postmodern self-reflexivity, typographical flamboyance, and unironic sentimentality. The work of George Saunders, meanwhile, though in many respects more contemporaneous with Wallace's work than that of these younger writers, also dovetailed with Wallace's own project. Meanwhile, Eggers's two literary magazine ventures, *McSweeneys* and *The Believer*, not only drew from Wallace's example for inspiration but also featured him and/or his work prominently and repeatedly.

As with the case of "E Unibus Pluram" and its program for a literary sensibility that might succeed traditional postmodernism, Wallace scholars have already addressed at great length the nature of Wallace's influence on this body of work, with Andrew Hoberek's "The Novel after David Foster Wallace" being perhaps the most succinct study of this sort. Hence, the current volume does not trace Wallace's artistic influence on the contemporary literary imagination. Rather, it registers a provocative pattern of *resistance* to Wallace's literary dominance. In keeping with Harold Bloom's language, this current volume traces what might be called Wallace *angst*. At one level, the degree to which these writers feel obliged to address Wallace directly testifies to that dominance. At the same time, by taking him on in the terms he set for himself, these writers simultaneously demythologize Wallace's persona and, in the process, carve out a place for themselves as worthy rivals.

This pattern of resistance works both fore and aft. In the first part, "Toward Wallace," I look at two key instances in which writers Wallace regarded as competitors anticipated many of the key ideas and literary strategies that he would later claim as his own. To borrow a concept associated with one of the writers treated here, these first two chapters serve as a gentle correction to the emerging conception of Wallace's breakthrough as largely singular and unprecedented. In the second part, I examine four novels published between 2006 and 2016—that is, published fully within the aura of the Wallace Effect—that address Wallace either directly or fictionally. All these works borrow Wallace's strategy, first introduced in "Westward," of staging an artistic rivalry between one author and another via a work of fiction that allegorizes that rivalry while also responding critically to the rival's work and its reception. I have tried to cast the essays as both parts of the text's ongoing exploration of the Wallace Effect and as free standing essays that readers can read separately in accordance with their own scholarly agendas. As a result, there is a small amount of unavoidable repetition that I hope those readers who take on the volume as a whole will forgive.

In the first chapter, I address John Barth's 1987 novel *The Tidewater Tales* and its companion work *Sabbatical*, tracing the numerous ways Barth adjusts his earlier metafictional strategies to account for many of the shortcomings Wallace would level at Barth in "Westward." This chapter, which supplements Charles Harris's recent essay, "The Anxiety of Influence: The John Barth/David Foster Wallace Connection," also traces elements in Barth's novel that suggest a deeper engagement with it than Wallace disclosed in his own pronouncements on Barth.

The second chapter discusses *Prisoner's Dilemma*, the second novel by Wallace's direct contemporary, and possibly most gifted rival, Richard Powers. Reading the novel alongside Richard Rorty's *Contingency, Irony, and Solidarity*, the essay teases out Powers's early articulation of a new literary sensibility that, as Powers explained, "is both metafictional and realistic" ("Art of Fiction" 113); in doing so, it argues that Powers also anticipated many of Wallace's programmatic directives, given that the novel appeared a year before "Westward" and five years before "E Unibus Pluram."

The second section, titled "The Wallace Effect," begins with a chapter focused on Jeffrey Eugenides' 2011 novel *The Marriage Plot*, which features a very Wallace-esque character named Leonard Bankhead. I read the novel's college love triangle as a coded battle with Wallace for artistic supremacy, wherein Eugenides pits Bankhead against an autobiographically conceived rival lover, both of whom compete for the novel's heroine, conceived here as an ideal reader.

Chapter 4 addresses Claire Messud's 2008 novel *The Emperor's Children*, which follows the romantic entanglements and literary ambitions of a group of Manhattan twentysomethings who invoke the "sad kids" of Wallace's target readership. The essay explores Messud's positive embrace of novelistic irony as well as the various ways this embrace responds to Wallace's critique of same.

Wallace is also a key figure in Jonathan Franzen's 2011 novel, *Freedom*, the focus of Chapter 5. This novel's love triangle features a womanizing punk rock musician named Richard Katz who sleeps with the wife of his best friend. Drawing upon Franzen's various accounts of his friendship with Wallace and his reaction to Wallace's suicide, the essay explores how the novel's love triangle allegorizes Franzen's relationship with Wallace, a relationship that Franzen has repeatedly described as frankly competitive.

The final chapter explores the burgeoning feminist reaction against Wallace's literary stature by way of a close reading of Lauren Groff's 2015 work *Fates and Furies.* The essay also examines Wallace's pop-culture persona and its possible impact on the growing resistance to *Infinite Jest*, as testified by Amy Hungerford's 2016 essay, "On Not Reading DFW."

PART ONE

Toward Wallace

1

Something Both and Neither

Marshes, Marriage, and the Fertile Invention of John Barth's *The Tidewater Tales*

An unabashedly ambitious writer, one haunted, as A. O. Scott intuited, by "a feeling of belatedness," David Foster Wallace signaled early on that he wished to join the pantheon of US postmodernist novelists, a group that includes Thomas Pynchon, William Gaddis, Don DeLillo, and John Barth (Scott 39). Yet he also wanted to move past those writers, to enact some advance on postmodern metafiction that would single him out as the most prominent figure in the movement, still unnamed, that would follow postmodernism. Of all his distinguished artistic precursors, Wallace chose John Barth as the one writer he would "take on" directly. As he famously admitted in 1993, "If I have a real enemy, a patriarch for my patricide, it's probably Barth and Coover and Burroughs, even Nabokov and Pynchon" (*Conversations* 48). Wallace's complaint with these writers focuses on their once innovative use of "self-consciousness and irony and archaism," which, he argues, "served valuable purposes . . . for their time" but have now been absorbed "by U.S. commercial culture," a process that "has had appalling consequences for writers and everyone else" (48). In Wallace's depiction of his own artistic predicament, if he was going to move successfully past the hegemony of self-consciousness and irony, he would have to clear artistic space for himself—that is, commit an "artistic patricide." Of the five writers he names as possible targets of this patricide, he reduced his murder victim to one, the first named. In the process, Wallace consciously elevated Barth into the embodiment of the brand of postmodernism his fiction would correct.

He committed this "patricide" in his 1989 novella "Westward the Course of Empire Takes Its Way," the concluding piece in his first story collection, *Girl with Curious Hair*. In the collection's copyright page, Wallace reveals that parts of the novella "are written in the margins of John Barth's 'Lost in the Funhouse' and Cynthia Ozick's 'Usurpation (Other People's Stories)'" (vi). The story's protagonist is an aspiring writer named Mark Nechtr who is enrolled in a graduate writing workshop taught by a one Professor Ambrose, author of the "big-deal story" "Lost in the Funhouse," which a maverick adman named J. D. Steelritter plans to transform into a national franchise of actual funhouses (243). Ambrose Mensch is the name of Barth's protagonist in "Lost in the Funhouse." Nechtr, an archery champion whom the story's narrator endows with "the kind of careless health so complete it's sickening," bears ambivalent feelings about his teacher (233). While he admits that Ambrose(/Barth) "exerts an enormous influence on [his] outlook," Nechtr "does not trust him . . . Even when he doesn't listen to [Ambrose], he's consciously reacting against the option of listening, and listens for what not to listen to" (292–93). For all of that, the story declares Necthr to be "the boy who would inherit academic fiction's orb and crown" and someone "hotly cocky enough to think he might someday inherit Ambrose's bald crown and ballpoint scepter, to wish to try and sing to the *next* generation of the very same kids" (335, 348). Near the end of the novella, the narrator outlines a breakthrough story Nechtr will someday write in which he fictionalizes himself as an archery champion named Dave.

I have written about this piece at greater length elsewhere and so will not rehearse that reading here (see *Understanding David Foster Wallace* 102–15). Nevertheless, this brief outline of Wallace's 150-page novella reveals the basic contours of the battle Wallace staged with his literary precursors. As Charles Harris and I have posited, Wallace conceived of his battle in terms of Harold Bloom's 1973 volume, *The Anxiety of Influence*. In Bloom's theory, aspiring poets—a term meant to include artistic writers more generally—create space for their own work by directly confronting the influence of their precursors. In the book's introduction, Bloom explains, "Poetic history . . . is held to be indistinguishable from poetic influence, since strong poets make that history by misreading one another, so as to clear imaginative space for themselves" (5). Bloom goes onto identify his theory with Freud, suggesting thereby that the relationship between aspirants, or ephebes, and their stronger antecedents is essentially Oedipal, wherein the younger poet must overcome, and in effect kill, the father, resulting in what Wallace frankly identified as a "patricide."

Although Wallace's story graphs so perfectly onto Bloom's theory so as to function as a deft parody of Bloom, this parodic strain does not diffuse Bloom's importance to Wallace's project. Rather, it enhances Wallace's objectives. Whereas Bloom's volume traces the battle of influence as a buried strain in poetic history that his readings disclose, Wallace, the belated writer who must work in the light of Bloom's own disclosures, employs Bloom self-consciously in a matter reminiscent of metafictional self-consciousness, the very feature he most envies and resents in the work of his chosen patriarch, Barth. "Westward" parodies both Barthian metafiction and Bloomian anxiety, all the while retaining the valence of each influence. And just to make sure his readers understood what he was about here, Wallace confirmed his debt to Bloom in the pages of *Infinite Jest* (cited as *IJ*), where he titles an imagined motion picture after a line from the Gnostic Gospels that Bloom uses as the title of his own prologue—namely, "It Was a Great Marvel That They Were in the Father without Knowing Him" (Bloom 3, *IJ* 992, n24).

According to D. T. Max, Wallace's biographer, Wallace had high hopes for "Westward." In a letter to his friend, the novelist Jonathan Franzen, he declared, "In my view [the story is] far and away the best piece of sustained fiction I've ever written" (Max 98). Conversely, Max reports that Franzen, like "nearly all of Wallace's friends, wondered why Wallace held 'Westward' in such special regard" (98). In any event, Wallace took the piece's modest impact as an early artistic blow. Yet the relative failure of "Westward" should not have been surprising to him, given that all of its programmatic directives for a fiction designed for "the

next generation of . . . sad kids" refer to work that has yet to be
written. Even Nechtr's breakthrough story is presented only in
outline. Wallace himself would later argue that the story was more a
ground-clearer than a stand-alone statement, an attempt to exhaust
Barthian metafiction's hold over him, to "get it over with, and then
out of the rubble reaffirm the idea of art being a living transaction
between humans" (*Conversations* 41).

Harris wryly notes that the novella has helped promote a "common
narrative"—or, more properly, "a myth"—regarding Wallace's
relationship to Barth. In that myth, Harris explains, "Wallace fell
under the influence of Barth and other postmodern writers, only
to wrest himself free of this sinister authority as he matured as a
writer, steering his own fiction away from its sway and becoming
one of postmodern fiction's strongest detractors" ("Anxiety" 103).
But the situation is more complex than that. Harris, who also reads
"Westward" as steeped in Harold Bloom's "anxiety" model of
artistic influence, suggests that the novella "is better understood as
agonistic" rather than "antagonistic" in its relationship with Barth's
fiction ("Anxiety" 104). Harris and I both deem the novella a "self-
consciously filial" *misprision*, that is, a deliberate *misreading* of
Barth. One of Wallace's most clear misreadings of Barth involves
a telling absence. Wallace described the novella as "written in the
margins of John Barth's 'Lost in the Funhouse,'" which is accurate
enough, and yet that laser focus on Barth's late 1960s work has also
invited Wallace's many champions to ignore the work Barth was
producing at the same time that Wallace was leveling his critique.
For although, as Harris shows, Wallace wants to introduce his own
work as "a fulfillment of the putatively unrealized possibilities of
Barth's fiction and postmodern fiction in general," Barth's fiction
of the late 1980s was already fulfilling many of the possibilities
Wallace wanted to claim as his own. Specifically, his 1987 novel,
The Tidewater Tales deftly embodies many of the qualities Wallace
felt Barth's fiction lacked and which his own fiction would amend.
What's more, Wallace's own writing of the period vividly betrays
his familiarity with the novels his critique pointedly ignores.

In "Westward," Wallace argues that Barth's metafiction is
essentially solipsistic and narcissistic. In making this critique,
he takes direct aim at one of Barth's most distinctive tropes, the
equation of storytelling with sex, a motif most spelled out in his
1972 novella collection *Chimera*. In Barth's early conception of the

model, the male author joins with the passive female reader, here figured as Dunyazade, sister of the *Arabian Nights'* Scheherazade, in a playful act of storytelling coitus. Barth himself assumes the role of a twentieth-century genie named Djean who travels back in time to the world of the *Arabian Nights*. Barth's genie double insists that the "teller's role . . . is essentially masculine, the listener's or reader's feminine, and the tale was the medium of their intercourse" (34). The genie goes on to explain that this erotic storytelling model was "potentially fertile for both partners . . . for it goes beyond male and female. The reader is likely to find herself pregnant with new images . . .; but the storyteller may find himself pregnant too" (34).

In "Westward," Wallace charges Barth's brand of postmodern metafiction as "untrue, as a lover" because "it can only reveal. Itself is its only object. It's the act of a lonely solipsist's self-love . . . It's lovers not being lovers. Kissing their own spine. Fucking themselves" (332). Furthermore, Wallace complains that "the poor lucky reader's not that scene's target" (332). The reader stands outside the text, watching it run through its self-reflexive contortions but remaining unengaged, unaroused. Conversely, Wallace wants to amend Barth's model by reprising and repurposing the "Funhouse" motif from the story collection that preceded *Chimera*. In Wallace's new conception of the postmodern text, the story itself would not be a funhouse, as in Barth's work, but rather would reside within a funhouse, where it waits to be discovered by a reader, here figured as "a lover." He goes on to urge, "Make the reader a lover, who wants to be inside. Then do him. Pretend the whole thing's like love" (331). Wallace's ideal postmodern text would "use metafiction as a bright smiling disguise" but still be directed at the reader rather than itself (333). It would be both self-reflexive and *other* directed.

What Wallace deliberately conceals is the fact that Barth was already obliquely addressing Wallace's critiques, even as Wallace was committing his patricide. *Tidewater Tales* not only anticipates Wallace's suggestion that Barth's erotic storytelling motif be amended to invite the lover into the narrative but also addresses and seeks to correct the inherent sexism of the model itself. What's more, the novel, in conjunction with its prequel *Sabbatical* (1982), signals Barth's pivot from the hyper-self-reflexive work of his first major phase, which concludes with his 1979 summative work *LETTERS*, to a new, outwardly focused metafiction, a shift identified by Thomas Carmichael as "a return to the discourse of the realistic enterprise" in Barth's corpus, a shift that Carmichael insists marks a decisive event in our "understanding of the course of the postmodern impulse in American culture" (329–30). The Barth Wallace was killing off had already been abandoned—by Barth himself.

It also does not do to suggest that Wallace was unfamiliar with the work his critique elides. For one thing, the format of "Westward the Course of Empire Takes Its Way" betrays a debt to *Tidewater Tales*. Throughout the novella, Wallace interrupts the narrative with bold-face section headings that run the gamut from one-line clauses— that is, "How They Know Each Other" (251)—to paragraph-long sentences that fill half the page (288). The format appears to be a nod to *Tidewater Tales'* playful section breaks, which also interrupt the text, comment upon it, and range from one-word interruptions to, in one case, a single sentence that runs for a page and a half and introduces a "section" that consists of a single word, "Ahem" (73).[1] "Here and There," a story included in *Girl with Curious Hair* alongside "Westward," features an innovative narrative point of view in which a young man and young woman narrate together the story of their doomed relationship, a dual, multigendered storytelling strategy that appears to owe a debt to *Tidewater Tales'* unique narrative point of view, which was in fact first introduced in *Sabbatical*, and which Barth has described as "the first person-duple voice of a well-coupled couple" (*Sabbatical* 3).[2]

Admittedly, these echoes are largely cosmetic. Nevertheless, they provide clues to Wallace's larger purpose in choosing Barth as the target of his patricide. As Harris points out, Wallace was

---

[1]Wallace would carry over this technique in *Infinite Jest*, starting with the introduction of Hal Incandenza's "First Extant Written Comment on Anything Even Remotely Filmic" (140) and continuing through the headers for the novel's account of the rise and fall of video phones, or videophony (144–45), and Mario's film about his brother Hal titled *Tennis and the Feral Prodigy* (172).

[2]Similarly, Harris suggests two instances in Wallace's work that betray a familiarity with *Sabbatical*. First, he observes that "a brutal gang rape with a whisky bottle" in Wallace's "Brief Interview (#46)" "echoes Barth's description of Miriam's rapes in *Sabbatical*" (108). Second, he suggests that an arrow possessed by "Westward"'s main character, Mark Nechtr, is "a nod, it would seem, to (*Sabbatical's*) Fenwick's mysteriously reappearing boina in *Sabbatical*," which, in turn, Barth intended as a "homage to Tyrone Slothrop's lost and found harmonica in Pynchon's *Gravity's Rainbow*" (*Further* 36; qtd. in Harris, "Anxiety" 110).

"probably aware" of these "elisions" but made them deliberately "to clear space for his own effort to extend and deepen the ethical dimensions in postmodern fiction" (107). Hence, the purpose of this essay is not to chastise Wallace for dishonesty. Rather, this essay seeks to give proper due to *Tidewater Tales* for correcting some of the excesses and errors of Barth's own tradition and telegraphing a number of tropes and advances that Wallace would work very hard to claim as largely his own.

About two-thirds of the way through *The Tidewater Tales*, Peter Sagamore, one-half of the husband-and-wife team who jointly narrates the action, finds himself in a precarious erotic predicament. While taking a naked morning swim in the Chesapeake Bay, which he and his wife Kate Sherritt have been exploring via their sailboat *Story*, he is unexpectedly joined by Leah Talbott, the equally naked wife of another sailing couple whose boat and narrative have intersected with that of Peter and his wife. As Talbott approaches him, he thinks, "The beauty of women, Donald Barthelme somewhere proposes, makes of adultery a painful duty," to which Peter adds, "Yes, well: And love makes of fidelity a manageable responsibility" (424). The scene and the novel both end without an illicit coupling by any of the four members of this quartet. Fidelity and equality prevail.

In collegially "correcting" the casual sexism of one of his most celebrated literary contemporaries, Barth enacts in miniature one of the overarching agendas at work in *The Tidewater Tales*. Although it is preceded in Barth's *oeuvre* by the similarly themed and narratively linked prequel *Sabbatical*, which this subsequent book in effect repossesses, *The Tidewater Tales* is Barth's most overtly feminist production. From its multigendered first-person narrative viewpoint to its rich network of images and symbols connecting story production to pregnancy, from its linking of male sexual violence with US imperialism and environmental exploration to its extended portrait of a successful, sexually equal married couple, the book can be seen as Barth's attempt not only to free the tradition of postmodern metafiction from its predominantly male lineage but also to "correct" the patriarchal biases that scaffolded some of his own earlier productions.

Barth was clearly stung by the charge of sexism, as testified by a brief piece he published in *Esquire* around the time of *Sabbatical* and which he republished in *The Friday Book* (*FB*). Written in response to an invitation from that magazine to "settle scores with some particularly scathing reviewer," Barth's brief entry ostensibly rejects the terms of the original invitation—"I am proof against invective," he declares early on—focuses its ire instead at a scathing review of John Hawkes's *The Blood Oranges,* but not before Barth recalls the "imperfectly suppressed fart who, in the columns of the *New York Review of Books,* called the author of *Chimera* a 'narrative chauvinist pig'" (*FB* 216). That "fart" was in fact Michael Wood, who concludes his unsympathetic review of Barth's 1972 novella collection by accusing Barth of "treating his work in the way that the heroes of *Chimera,* confronted with Amazons and other liberated ladies, learn not to treat women. He is a narrative chauvinist pig" (Wood 35).

The charge is a complex one, to be sure: Wood argues that, in hiding behind pastiche and parody, Barth produces books that are deliberately unequal to the "brilliant mind" that produced them. Nevertheless, in characterizing this alleged self-sabotage as the strategy of a "narrative chauvinist pig," Wood makes an even broader charge that goes to the heart of one of *Chimera*'s governing tropes—namely, the equation of storytelling with sex, as already noted. Charles Harris argues that the metaphor is "not sexist, . . . for the audience does not assume a passive or inferior role" (*Passionate* 131). As the genie explains, "Narrative . . . was a love-relation, not a rape: its success depended upon the reader's consent and co-operation, which she could withhold or at any moment withdraw; also upon her own combination of experience and talent for enterprise, and the author's ability to arouse, sustain, and satisfy her interest" (*Chimera* 26). As Harris argues, Barth's genie culls his tales from the *Arabian Nights,* and "thus from Scheherazade, so their roles and accompanying genders are immediately reversed" (131). But these caveats do not solve Barth's problem, for his model requires female storytellers to adopt an "essentially masculine" role in order to achieve authority. However one might want to spin it, Barth's argument reinscribes what Sandra Gilbert and Susan Gubar identify as "the patriarchal notion that the writer 'fathers' his text just as God fathered the world" (4), a notion that Edward Said argues, in "The Novel as Beginning Intention," is inextricable from the word "author" itself. Citing the *Oxford English Dictionary,* Said notes that the word "author" implies "a person who originates or gives existence to something, a begetter, father, or ancestor, a person who sets forth written statements" (83, qtd. Gilbert and Gubar 4). Well-meaning though it is, Barth's trope nevertheless sustains what Gilbert and Gubar call the "metaphor of literary paternity." The pen remains a figurative penis in this trope, and despite the genie's assertion, which goes unsupported, that the model "goes beyond male and female," gender binaries remain firmly in place. No wonder the charge of "narrative chauvinist pig" stayed with him.

But not unproductively.

Despite Wood's drubbing, *Chimera* went on to win the National Book Award (it was Barth's third nomination). No such happy fate greeted the work that originally contained *Chimera* and which overtly closed out what Barth identified as the First Phase of his Career—namely, 1979's mammoth *LETTERS*. By reprising the characters and themes from his first six books and weaving them together into a complex unity, *LETTERS* serves as an authoritative commentary upon, as well as a rich artistic summation of, his entire literary career up to that point. Unfortunately, the novel also foregrounds, even more so than the six previous novels it synthesizes and completes, the troubling pattern of sexism that marred those otherwise remarkable early novels. Of the six primary letter writers who jointly author this "Old-Time Epistolary Novel" (the seventh writer being the author himself), five are male characters from Barth's previous five books (excepting *Chimera*, his sixth). The remaining letter writer is a one Lady Amherst, the novel's most important "new" character who, given her erotic history with numerous European modernist authors (James Joyce, Aldous Huxley, Hermann Hesse, Evelyn Waugh), is figured as the "Fair Embodiment of the Great Tradition" (*LETTERS* 39).

Although Lady Amherst is the novel's most prolific letter writer (twenty-six letters in all) and hence the novel's leading narrative voice, her largely ignominious fate in the novel's labyrinthine plot parallels that of the half a dozen other secondary female characters who drift in and out of the various letters. For the duration of *LETTERS*, the loquacious, verbally flamboyant Lady Amherst remains erotically submissive to Ambrose Mensch, the brooding, self-absorbed hero of Barth's *Lost in the Funhouse*. Her early letters consist of floridly pornographic descriptions of her marathon intercourse sessions with Amrbose, to which she consents "for no better reason than that persisting in refusal becomes too much bother" (63). Her letters from the novel's mid-section detail her extended humiliation as Ambrose conducts a flagrant affair with Bea Golden, née Jeannine Mack (originally seen as a young girl in *The Floating Opera*, about whom more anon), while her late letters record her passive acceptance of said affair and of Ambrose's return to her bed, where they set about trying to get pregnant. As for Bea Golden/Jeannine Mack, she is passed carelessly between Reg Prince, a radical film director, and Ambrose, who both use her as a proxy spoil in their war between "Director and Author," after which she is tossed aside and possibly raped by Jerome Bray (a descendant of *Giles Goat-Boy*'s Giles Stoker) before she turns up, broken and humiliated, on the deck of the *Osbourne Jones*, the sailboat owned and manned by *The Floating Opera*'s Todd Andrews, who might possibly be her father and with whom she conducts several acts of possibly "cordial incest" before she is, in fact, anally raped by Andrews (see 707). Andrew subsequently dismisses her from his boat; our last glimpse of her is as an abandoned drug addict in Jerome Bray's nefarious clutches (*LETTERS* 747).

The novel's two other primary female characters fare no better. In *Lost in the Funhouse* (*LF*), Ambrose famously finds washed up on the shore of the Chesapeake Bay a bottle that contains a one-page message, the top of which reads, "TO WHOM IT MAY CONCERN" and the bottom of which concludes "YOURS TRULY," with the middle of the page remaining blank (*LF* 56). Although an unnamed spouse makes an oblique appearance in the Ambrose-authored metafiction "Title" from that same volume, we do not learn much about Ambrose's married life in the book that launches him as a character. Conversely, in *LETTERS*, that wife is revealed to be a charmless, vindictive woman named Marsha Blank, "mind and character to match," to whom Ambrose is drawn primarily because of "her name" (239); in other words, she is the "blank" he has been trying to "fill" since receiving his cryptic water message as a young boy. After she leaves him, Marsha becomes an insatiable nymphomaniac nicknamed Pocahontas who is said "would unman a regiment of rapists" (100), only to become, like Jeanine Mack, a drug addict, victim of Jerome Bray's sexual violence, and, eventually, the passive wife of *The End of the Road*'s Jacob Horner. On their wedding night she is forced against her inclinations into submissive sexual intercourse with that same novel's Joseph Morgan in exchange for a narcotic fix, all in order to "settle the score" for Horner's affair, seventeen years earlier, with Morgan's deceased wife Remmie. As for Merope Bernstein, one of the novel's rare new female characters, Bray somehow deflates her buttocks, which are commented upon throughout the novel and deemed "uncomely" by Andrews (731), before turning her into another drug addict, but not before she, like Jeanine, is passed around from various male lovers, Reg Prince and Bray among them.

While this catalog hardly captures the rich texture and complex allegorical and symbolic substructure governing *LETTERS*'s elaborate design, it is also not inaccurate. The novel's female characters are by and large reduced to sexual objects and callously mistreated throughout. Wallace's infamous 1998 takedown of John Updike, Norman Mailer, and Philip Roth as the US fiction's representative "Great Male Narcissists" and misogynistic "phallocrats" applies equally well to the Barth of *LETTERS* (Wallace, *Lobster* 51, 53). That being said, *LETTERS,* though published in 1979, is very much a 1960s novel. The book is set in March–September 1969 and features hippies, drugs, college radicals, riots, revolutions, the moon landing, the Ted Kennedy Chappaquidick scandal, and the Vietnam War. It is telling to remember that 1969 was also the year of Philip Roth's *Portnoy's Complaint*, "Penelope Ashe's" *Naked Came the Stranger*, Irving Wallace's *The Seven Minutes*, and Vladimir Nabokov's incest-addled *Ada*. In its original conception, *LETTERS* was very much swinging with the times. Barth apparently began the work not long after publishing *Lost in the Funhouse* (1968) but ran into difficulty early on. The concluding two novellas in *Chimera* were originally planned for *LETTERS*: Ambrose spends most of the latter novel making notes for "Perseid," which notes he then bequeaths to the "Author" along with instructions for said Author to publish that novella and its two companion pieces before proceeding with the epistolary novel already underway (*LETTERS* 652–53). Following *Chimera*, Barth returned to his magnum opus and grimly saw it through to its tidy but protracted end. In a promotional interview published in the *Boston Globe*'s Sunday magazine, he revealed that it "took my whole fucking forties" to produce the book (*FB* 177). By the time these backdated letters finally arrived at their destination, the original occupants had moved on.

Understandably, *LETTERS*'s critical and commercial failure must have hit Barth hard. Even more remarkable is how quickly, and thoroughly, he rallied from this blow. The US culture had

changed remarkably in the ten years between *LETTERS*'s original
conception and its fruition, but so had Barth's circumstances.
When he began the novel, he was recently divorced, at the height
of his writerly fame, and, as a college professor, a direct eye
witness to the High Sixties, as he calls them. As he relates in his
memoir essay "Teacher," "More than once I returned from some
teargassed campus to find mine 'trashed,' on strike, or cordoned
off by gas-masked National Guardsmen" (*Further* 10). In winter
1969, Shelly Rosenberg, a former star student from his early-1960s
tenure at Pennsylvania State University, showed up at a lecture he
was delivering at Boston College, and Barth fell in love. The two
married several years later and moved to Baltimore. "You opened
my eyes," he writes to Shelly in "Teacher"; "You changed my life"
(*Further* 18).[3]

    Tidewater Tale's narrative situation introduces a number of key
revisions to Barth's earlier storytelling model. Although the novel is
surfeited with sexuality, its basic storytelling situation is not erotic per
se. Rather, Barth develops a new model in which storytelling is a joint
project by two equally matched and complementary participants, one
male and one female. The woman storyteller does not need to assume
a masculine role in order to contribute, nor does the man have to
assume the female role to listen. Role reversal is no longer necessary
in this new narrative situation. The stories that emerge are not the
"medium of their intercourse" but rather the "product" of them, a
"Combining" of the male and female, but also a "Consumption" and
"Union of Contraries" that, like the sperm and egg that form a new
organism, yields "Something Both and Neither" (386). As the woman
tells her husband early on, "You tell your water under the bridge, and
I'll tell mine, if we're really going to do this. It should be a team effort,
like pregnancy" (96).

    Barth depicts his dual narrators as a complementary pair.
Both narrators are exactly thirty-nine years old. In a nod to his
earlier trope, the male, Peter Sagamore, is writer, while the female,
Katherine Sherritt, is a professional "reader" in the sense that she
is a librarian. But in this case, Peter, despite his last name, which

---

[3] Barth provides a more thorough account of his and Shelly's remeet and subsequent
marriage in *Once Upon a Time: A Floating Opera*. See 364–80.

might be glossed as "saga more," or *continue to tell tales*,[4] is a blocked writer whose work has become increasingly minimalist to the point of silence, while Katherine is not only physically energetic and nimbly athletic—"an Outward bound type, Kath: backpacker, white-water canoeist, distance swimmer" (30)—but also eight and half months pregnant with twins. Peter comes from a blue-collar background and is essentially self-taught; Katherine is a blue-blood WASP packed with privilege. In every respect, these two form a perfect yin and yang, or, to use a trope from the novel, two caskets each of which contains the key to the other. Thinking back to their first meeting, Katherine "felt she'd felt . . . that center of energy beneath P's laid-back manner, the dark small nothinghood beneath her animation. And that center of his had filled and swelled that center of her; hers had actively received, accommodated, enfolded his" (120). Among many other things, *Tidewater Tales* is the *Moby-Dick* of parallelism.

According to the tradition of "literary paternity" traced out in Gilbert and Gubar, Peter's literary silence would constitute a symbolic "castration," that is, a loss of the pen/penis. But Peter is anything but a eunuch: his devotion to his wife Kath is both spiritual and sexual, and his ardor for her remains undimmed from first to last. Besides, he has just fathered twins. Clearly, Peter's pen isn't his problem. But his impending fatherhood might be. Although both he and Kath understand that "Less is More antedates our pregnancy" and hope that Peter's writer's block "and our pregnancy will at worst reach term together," they both nevertheless worry about "the unthinkable burden [his silence] will place upon our parenthood if, to our dismay, his art turns out to have been sacrificed upon that altar" (55, 56). Peter is not "fathering" texts that he then leaves to his "reader" to raise. Rather, in the same way that they are jointly "producing" the story we are reading, he and his wife have produced children whom they will raise in a shared, equal partnership, the burden of which effort might in fact further impede his literary production. Barth does more than reverse the age-old connection between male sexual fecundity and artistic production.

---

[4]Berndt Clavier, in *John Barth and Postmodernism: Spatiality, Travel, Montage*, similarly speculates that Sagamore's name might be derived from the German *sag mehr*, which translates to "say more" (173).

He also breaks the gender binary that would assign concern about the incompatibility of parenthood and authorship solely to the mother. Nathan Zuckerman never worried about this stuff.

The novel's ingenious narrative point of view, the afore cited "first person-duple voice of a well-coupled couple" (*Sabbatical* 3),[5] also revises the storyteller/listener dynamic affirmed in *Chimera*'s Sherehezade narrative. Both Peter and Katherine "narrate" the novel in unison, to each other but also separately. They use the first-person plural when the narrative provides exposition, and their proper names when they each speak separately, usually but not always to each other. Peter is termed "the man of us," Katherine "the woman of us." At one point in the telling, Kath "swears to Christ we've become one person: Siamese twins, joined at the imagination" (401). Each partner, as Stan Fogel and Gordon Slethaug put it, "is teller and listener narrator and reader" (198). Their tale is a Hegelian synthesis of their thesis/antithesis. As per Wallace's suggestion from "Westward," Barth has effectively brought the figure of the "reader" into the text, such that reader and writer, auditor and storyteller, are combined in a fluctuating yin and yang.

The words we're reading, however, are not necessarily the words they say to each other. Many of the stories, particularly those involving their shared past, are only hinted at on the boat: Peter and Katherine don't need to tell those stories in detail because they both know them well enough already. "How much of this do we literally say, in this articulated wise?" they ask early on. The answer is, not much. In the novel's extended prologue, Peter and Katherine recall the old prison joke in which the inmates have numbered all their jokes to save themselves the trouble of having to tell them outright. When a new inmate shouts a random number and no one laughs, one of the old-timers shrugs and says, "Some people just can't tell a joke" (70).[6] The prison-joke sequence clues us into one of the key

---

[5]In this same foreword, Barth observes that this "first-person duple voice" is a narrative viewpoint "that I believe myself to have invented" (*Sabbatical* 3).

[6]Peter adds a Barthian twist on this old joke by having the joke that flops be the joke about the prisoners who numbered their jokes. Conversely, Kath tells a version in which the newcomer yells a random number ("Thirty-nine!") and is greeted by guffaws, to which the old-timer explains, "We never heard that one before" (72). The two variations of the joke nod back to Barth's "Literature of Exhaustion" and "Literature of Replenishment," respectively; in Peter's version, the joke's narrative

features of the narrative we're reading. As Pete and Katherine tell
their stories to each other and pick up new stories from various
passersby, they "code" these tales as entries in their ship log. Kath
insists that Peter

> *not* write down these tales and dreams and anecdotes. Not
> yet. Why not let's dream and tell, tell and dream, narrate and
> navigate whither listeth wind and tide until we are delivered of
> our posterity, or about to be, and *then*—by when you'll be about
> to burst as I am—deliver yourself of our several stories, duly
> arted up. (169)

Like the prisoners with their numbered jokes, Peter jots down brief
reminders of the tales and dreams they experience along the way,
each entry a mnemonic aid to help Peter write the novel we're
reading, an event that happens off page, after the telling. These same
one-line entries will later serve as the numerous subheadings that
break up the blocks of narrative, the whole list of which is printed
at the beginning of the novel as the nine-page table of contents.

   Harris notes that Barth's *LETTERS* would constitute what
Steven Kellman calls "a self-begetting novel," that is "a novel the
central action of which is the process of its own composition"
(Harris 163–64). In Wallace's conception, *LETTERS* fails to fulfill
the storytelling-as-lovemaking trope because it is "untrue" to its
erotic partner, the reader. *LETTERS* can only offer readers the
spectacle of its author "fucking himself" (332). And, to be sure,
the largest collection of letters—namely, those by Lady Amherst—is
addressed directly to the author, who briefly addresses all of the
other characters, all of whom in turn write to various characters
from their own narratives. Only two short letters, which appear
at the beginning and end, respectively, are addressed to the reader.
For the rest of the novel, the poor lucky reader is not these letters'
addresee. Conversely, Wallace calls for a fiction that opens itself
to the reader; the story itself "should treat the reader like it wants
to . . . well, fuck him" (331). *Tidewater Tales* achieves that aim, as
its narrative is the product of a form of love making undertaken by

---

has been exhausted, leaving behind only its form, whereas in Katherine's version
this state of exhaustion proves to be the ground for an unexpected replenishment.

its two narrators who are both tellers and readers simultaneously. Peter and Katherine jointly experience the action and thus produce the stories that will later be transformed into the language we are reading. As Susan Seckler, in the similarly structured *Sabbatical* puts it, "The interruption of our voyage begins our writing" (*Sabbatical* 365). Male and female, sperm and egg, join to produce a third thing, the tale, that is something both and neither; that tale, once "delivered," is then authored into language, and that language will produce a narrative that, like the "tale" that inspired it, ends at its own beginning, forming yet another Barthian Möbius strip that replicates the endlessly repeating narrative that served as the "content" of Barth's first such strip, offered as a *Sgt. Pepper*–like "cut out" in the opening pages of *Lost in the Funhouse*: "Once upon a time there was a story that began once upon a time" and so on, ad infinitum. With this same magical incantation, Odysseus and Nausicaa, in "The Long True Story of Odysseus's Short Last Voyage," manage to escape human time and enter into the timelessness of the narrative tradition, such that they sail into the novel's 1980 Chesapeake Bay and, in disguise, tell this story to Peter and Katherine, "the principal characters of a work of fiction entitled *The Tidewater Tales*" (239), whose similar narrative immortality is possible only when they get transformed into fictional characters but not while they spin their tale. "What you're reading, reader, is P's and K's *story*," they remind us early on. "But what husband and wife are living, and trying rather desperately just now without success to read ahead in, is not their story. It's their life" (140). Only when their story is told and *then* written down can they reverse thrust on time's arrow, but that story is their story and not their life.

Tidewater Tales' fertile narrative form also revises *LETTERS*'s much more rigid formalism. In his Heideggerean reading of the latter, Harris argues that Barth's approach to the external world, that is the world prior to novelistic representation, can be compared to Heidegger's concept of *Dasein*, the latter of which "draws together past, present, and future, *res extensa* and *res cogitans*, into a reciprocal totality" (185). Similarly, in *LETTERS*, Barth "proposes a language that *discloses* rather than represents the world, yet which acknowledges that the world has no existence apart from our poetic 'saying' of it"; Harris adds that this approach to novelistic representation achieves "a balance between form and flux" (185). Whereas *LETTERS*, with its elaborate calendar/title structure and preordained arrangement of epistles, is more form than flux, *Tidewater Tales* reverses this dialectic in ways that might be read as an additional component of its feminizing agenda. The novel boasts three different title pages. The first appears where most title pages would appear, at the beginning. The second title page appears after the eighty-two-page prologue, the latter of which is titled "Our Story." This second title page adds two subtitles: *Or Whither the Wind Listeth, or Our House's Increase: A Novel.* Both subtitles refer to the novel's gestation. Peter and Katherine undertake their fortnight voyage with no plan, no map, no sense even that the trip will continue for fourteen days, as their journey is at every moment subject to interruption by the onset of Katherine's twin delivery. As such, the two sail randomly around their beloved Cheseapeake, wandering whither the wind listeth and absorbing into their growing narrative whatever they encounter along the way. As with Heidegger's *Dasein*, the narrative here neither resists nor embraces the chaos of the external world, to employ Harris's terms; rather, "the terms of the dilemma are simply *transcended*" (Harris 185). The external world enters the text in the form of "actual" weather events, news items, and "real" people such as Katherine Ann Porter and CIA agent John Paisley; these "real" objects merge, sperm to egg, with the novel's imaginative formal elements and produce a third thing that is, once again, both and neither. After the journey is done, Barth concludes the book by reprinting the original title page one more time on a left-facing page, which is also the novel's final page, suggesting the novel is both "finished" in its telling and now ready to begin in its writing. "That FINIS is only the beginning," as Kath remarks at the beginning of their journey and their novel, "On with our story?" (89).

What does any of this have to do with what I'm calling the novel's "feminizing agenda"? At the beginning of the novel's two major sections, Barth reprints a detailed map of the Chesapeake Bay. On one level, the maps help readers get their bearings as Peter and Katherine navigate whither the wind takes them. But the maps also invite a more formally pertinent interpretation. Here, we should first look at this novel's "dark twin," *Sabbatical*, for guidance and clarity. On that novel's title page, Barth includes a curious circle image bisected by a Y figure, in the middle of which resides a small oval. Heide Zeigler suggests that the image "represents, first, the egg which, after coming down one of the two fallopian tubes, is met by the sperm coming up the vagina" (83). In *Sabbatical*, the well-coupled narrators are not sure if they want children, which is a problem given that the woman, Susan, is secretly pregnant. Late in the novel, she unilaterally, though not without serious regret, aborts the child, leading the man, Fenn, to proclaim, "[T]his story, our story, it's our house and our child" (356–57), a formulation that pleases Fenn, who already has actual children by another marriage, but understandably leaves childless Susan considerably less consoled. As such, Zeigler argues that the abstract figure on the title page also "means the story as substitute for the child" (83). The twinned maps of the Cheseapeake Bay in *Tidewater Tales* function similarly as more organic and less formal representations of Peter and Katherine's near-term twin pregnancy. The fork that separates the Potomac River and the Chesapeake Bay itself represents the fallopian tubes, with the paisley figure of their boat, called significantly *Story*, representing both the sperm and the egg that have now been joined, male and female, blam and blooey. *Story* is both their boat and their dual narration but not their life. *Contra* Fenwick Turner, the expectant Peter proclaims (in one of the novel's bold, all cap subheadings), "A STORY IS NOT A CHILD" (410).

These two visual images also correspond to the fascinating ways in which *Sabbatical* connects to *The Tidewater Tales*. In terms of plot, the two novels link up via a message in a bottle that the two protagonists from the earlier novel send out to their doppelgängers in the latter, a sperm that finds its egg and hence joins the two novels such that they become something that is, again, both and neither. According to Barth's foreword to *Sabbatical*, the curious two-act play, *SEX EDUCATION: Play*, that floats to *Story* was originally to be included in the earlier novel, creating what Barth envisioned as a "Siamese twin of a book"; the plan proved unworkable, however, and so, "as happens with a fair percentage of twin pregnancies, the weaker sibling expired *in utero*" (3). In *Tidewater Tales*, Fenwick Turner and Susan Seckler reappear as Frank and Leah Talbott. What's more, we learn that Fenn/Frank wrote *SEX EDUCATION*'s first two acts but chose not to complete the third (*Tidewater Tales* 409). Instead, he and Susan bundled the two acts into a pair of canisters and sent them into the Chesapeake's fertile water, where they floated to fertile Peter and Katherine.

Fogel and Slethaug explore at length the various ways in which these two novels operate as "twinned" narratives and argue persuasively that "they must be viewed together" (192). Yet the two novels do not form yet another binary, yet another thesis/ antithesis, for the simple reason that one can read *Sabbatical* on its own, whereas *Tidewater Tales*, in both its actual conception and in its plot, has been "birthed" from the earlier narrative. In his foreword, Barth reveals that his original title for the earlier novel was *Sex Education and Sabbatical* (3), suggesting not only that the play was to occupy a major part of the narrative but also that it was to be a text-within-the-text that Fenn was composing while also jointly narrating with his wife the frame tale, a situation that Frank, in *Tidewater Tales* (*TT*), confirms, insofar as we can trust the proclamations of a fictional character (*TT* 415). In this scenario, then, Frank Talbott abandons the play but finishes the novel that is now available to us as *Sabbatical* in the same way that Barth abandoned his idea to include the play within that novel. In sending the play to Peter and Katherine, Frank replicates Barth's own composition process, by which the earlier novel provides the "seed" for the other. As it happens, Frank includes within the same canister his *boina*, which he wears while writing (as does Fenn in *Sabbatical*), and a paisley scarf. In *Sabbatical*, Fenn observes that "those paisley things looked like fat spermatozoa" (204). Ergo, the canister is both a fertilized egg and a message in a bottle, a container and the thing contained, a treasure the key to which is the treasure.

We can also read *SEX EDUCATION: Play* as a subtle revision of some of Barth's earlier riffs on narrative and sexuality. Fogel and Slethaug point out that the play represents another "self-conscious, intertextual relationship," this time between *Tidewater Tales* and "Night-Sea Journey," the more-or-less opening story of *Lost in the Funhouse* (200). Whereas "Night-Sea Journey" offers up a clever parody of existentialism and Cold War fear of global annihilation, *SEX EDUCATION* is frankly political in its concerns. In the former story, an anxious sperm swims furiously toward its goal, speculating all the while on the purpose of all this otherwise pointless swimming and of the vast genocide that will eliminate its fellow "swimmers." Conversely, *SEX EDUCATION* foregrounds the plight of a pair of eggs named June and May, who fret about the prospect of rape and loss of identity. Both *Sabbatical* and *Tidewater Tales* include brutally unflinching accounts of rape and sexual violence. "The Story of Miriam's *Other* Rapes" occupies fourteen devastating pages of *Sabbatical*, while "The Forest-Green Recrayoning of Mrs.

Porter Baldwin, Jr." takes up sixteen even denser pages of *Tidewater Tales*. What's more, Katherine's rapist, her congressman husband Porter Baldwin, later participates in an elaborate scheme to dump toxic waste in hers and Peter's beloved Chesapeake Bay, thereby linking the environmental destruction to male sexual violence.[7] Of *SEX EDUCATION*, Katherine "declares it to be the queerest mix of sophomoric and serious" (161), and, to be sure, much of the play's humor is juvenile and obvious: Woody Allen already made most of these same jokes in *Everything You Wanted to Know about Sex*. Conversely, the issues to which the play gives birth could not be any more serious, or real.

As Peter and Katherine read the play in unison, their comments about the unfolding story, as well as their remarks to each other, get incorporated into the "Play" as it appears on the pages of *Tidewater Tales*, rendering the text as permeable as the eggs that float toward their fate. Similarly, the "real" story of CIA agent John Paisley "permeates" the fictional membrane of both *Sabbatical* and *Tidewater Tales*, to the extent that the former novel reprints pages and pages of actual newspaper accounts regarding the case and the latter novel has Paisley's bloated corpse bump against Peter's and Katherine's boat. Here Barth introduces yet another binary that he seeks both to join and transcend—namely, that of seriousness and "play." It is not accidental, for instance, that the play's subtitle lacks a definite article. Although, as already noted, the narrators of *Tidewater Tales* insist that "Katherine Sherritt and Peter Sagamore are principally the principal characters in a work of fiction," they also insistently remind us that "the Chesapeake Bay is real, so are all the federal government operations on and around it," and "so was the corpse [of John Paisley] our *Story* ran into several cruises back on Sunday, 1 October 1978" (239). Paisley, whose name invokes one of Fenn's "fat spermatozoa," enters both novels as a means by which the texts can address serious issues regarding US foreign policy and international skullduggery, while also serving as yet another part of both novel's fictional play. One of the novel's CIA agents observes that "our kind may tell you six true things, as subsequently verified, in order to set you up for believing a seventh thing, which may be false" (249), a strategy that also applies to a writer of "realistic" fiction, such as *Tidewater Tales'* CIA narratives. And yet, in the case of the CIA one is not dealing with a "mixture of fiction and truth, but of facts and lies" (237). In this way, Barth fulfills a desire his genie expresses in *Chimera* to compose "longish tales which would take their sense from one another in several ways . . . and, if they were successful . . ., manage to be seriously, even passionately, *about* some things as well" (28).

In his oblique description in "Westward" of the kind of fiction that would follow that of Barth, Wallace, contra the Barth of *Lost in the Funhouse,* argues, "A story can, yes, . . . be made out of a Funhouse. But not by using the Funhouse as the kind of symbol you can take or leave standing there": rather, as touched upon earlier in this essay, he insists, "The way to make a story a Funhouse is to put the story itself in one. For a lover. Make the reader a lover, who wants to be inside" (*Girl* 331). In charging Barth's Funhouse as the site of "the lonely solipsist's self love," Wallace clearly had in mind Barth's description of the funhouse mirror-room: "In the funhouse mirror-room," Barth writes, "you can't see yourself go on forever, because no matter how you stand, your head gets in the way" (*Girl* 332, *LF* 85). Wallace replaces Barth's mirror metaphor with a new motif drawn from his hero Mark Nechtr's sport of choice, archery. He first describes a phenomenon governing the physics of shooting an arrow: to hit a target, he explains, archers must aim "a bit left of center, because of the dimensions of the bow": the whistling arrow then "zigzags, moving . . . alternately left and right, though in *ever diminishing amounts,* . . . until at a certain point the arrow, aimed with all sincerity just West of the lover, is on line with his heart" (333). In a clear nod to Barth, Nechtr explains that the left-of-center aim is necessitate by the fact that "the bow gets in the way" (293). Since in both Barth and Wallace the lover is the reader, Wallace's arrow confirms that this post-Barth fiction would be other directed, aimed beyond the text to the site of its reception. Barth's innovative strategy in *Tidewater Tales* antedates Wallace's directive on several levels. Far from representing "the lonely solipsist's self-love," *Tidewater Tales* opens the doors of Barth's own Funhouse and sends the narrative and its paired narrators, lovers both, on an outwardly directed journey that can be compared favorably to Wallace's arrow motif. Where Kate and Peter go is not the point;

the novel's pleasure results from the stories they tell along the way. The reader is on that boat, which, after all, is called *Story*. Hence, the novel's rich assortment of self-contained tales along the way, as well as its luxuriant affirmation of the pleasure of pure storytelling itself, fulfills Wallace's call for a fiction in which "the stuff the place is *made* of would make it Fun" (332).

Based on the example of *Tidewater Tales*, one is hard-pressed to think of another male novelist of Barth's generation and stature who so enthusiastically responded to the challenges of 1970s and 1980s feminism. Philip Roth dug in his heels; John Updike made matters worse by drawing bewildering connections between feminism and Hawthornean witchcraft; Thomas Pynchon stayed mum. Barth, on the other hand, perhaps drawing energy and inspiration from his to-all-accounts happy second marriage, not only tweaked his own work but also developed an entirely new aesthetic grounded in a model of gender equality that is light years removed from the lonely, solipsistic, and insistently male world of Nathan Zuckerman and Harry Angstrom—the same solipsistic world Wallace sought to puncture.

2

The Awful Way Back to We

Crackpot Realism and Ironic Liberalism in Richard Powers's *Prisoner's Dilemma*

Like Wallace, Richard Powers writes fiction that is palpably haunted by the legacy of postwar metafiction and the thunderous impact on the social sciences of continental poststructuralism. Rather than write passively within the nimbus of these dominant forces, however, Wallace and Powers seek to escape the insularity and self-reflection of postwar narrative art and its attendant body of criticism, all while honoring the indelible shifts in consciousness brought about by the postmodernity and literary theory. As explored earlier, Wallace, the most visible member of the "post-postmodern" generation, proposed a new approach to literary fiction that combined metafictional self-reflexivity and earnest openness. In a similar but generally unheralded move, Powers, in his second novel *Prisoner's Dilemma* (1988), seeks to reinvigorate the literary novel's engagement with the broader culture by constructing a decidedly pragmatic adaptation of poststructuralist anti-metaphysics that dovetails strikingly with the work of Richard Rorty, most particularly Rorty's nearly contemporary work, *Contingency, Irony, and Solidarity*. Much the way Wallace articulated his new approach as a joining of cynicism (self-consciousness, irony) and naiveté (earnestness, sincerity), Powers terms his solution to metafictional insularity "Crackpot Realism," a guardedly hopeful call for social reengagement and liberal hope that resonates with Rorty's vision of an ironic liberalism, one that marries a private rejection of final vocabularies with a push for liberal solidarity "constructed out of little pieces, rather than found already waiting, in the form of an ur-language that all of us recognize when we hear it" (Rorty 94). In both Wallace and Powers, the claims of poststructuralism are both honored and overcome via a pragmatic affirmation of usefulness within a larger suspicion of metaphysical certainty. Less widely appreciated is the fact that Powers sounded this call in 1988, whereas Wallace finally clarified his own set of ideas five years later, in 1993. Although Wallace's proposed solutions to the limits of postmodern self-reflexivity have achieved cultural prominence, Powers's own take on the problem both antedates and amplifies Wallace's arguments. This essay aims to give Powers his due in this regard.

Like most of Powers's fiction, *Prisoner's Dilemma* is an intricately constructed work built from a number of intertwining narrative strands. The book's central story line concerns the Hobsons, an American family living in DeKalb, Illinois, in the late 1970s. The family's brilliant but disturbed patriarch, Eddie Hobson, is a failed high school history teacher who, in the late fall and winter of 1978, has arrived at the terminal end of a mysterious illness that appears to be the result of radiation poisoning contracted when Eddie, while serving on the home front in New Mexico at the tail end of the Second World War, steps outside for a smoke and accidentally witnesses the first test detonation of the atomic bomb in Los Alamos. Interwoven with the events of that fateful fall are two additional narrative lines. One line traces a fanciful alternative history, created by Eddie up on his room, in which Walt Disney springs from prison ten thousand Americans of Japanese ancestry who were interred following the Pearl Harbor attack and puts them to work on a massively ambitious Frank Capra-like film called *You Are the War* that Disney hopes will save the world from destruction. The other narrative strand consists of a series of taped monologues in which the oldest Hobson, a twenty-five-year-old law student named Artie, records his memories of his father. From these three disparate but intimately linked narratives, Powers stages a complex inquiry into the individual's impact on, and possible complicity with, the larger global forces of mass destruction set in motion with Second World War, what the novel collectively refers to as the Big Picture. Within this broad and ambitious agenda, Powers has also encoded a compelling diagnosis and cure for postmodern irony that firmly anticipates the much more celebrated ideas proposed by Wallace five years after *Prisoner's Dilemma*'s 1988 publication.

Although Powers is generally regarded as a key figure in the post-postmodern turn, he does not get nearly as much credit as Wallace for being one of its earliest architects. Two factors account for this anomaly: first is the quality and stature of the novels Powers would go on to publish, a list that includes *The Gold-Bug Variations, Galatea 2.2, Plowing the Dark, The Time of Our Singing*, and *The Echo Maker*; second is the cult that has cohered around Wallace. In the immediate aftermath of *Infinite Jest*'s arrival, numerous scholars noted a natural affinity between Wallace's work and that of Powers, as evidenced by Tom LeClair's groundbreaking essay, "The Prodigious Fiction of Richard Powers, William Vollman, and David Foster Wallace," which examines all three writers as the natural heirs to Thomas Pynchon. LeClair, however, matches *Infinite Jest* not with *Prisoner's Dilemma* but with Powers's 700-page encyclopedic novel, *The Gold-Bug Variations*, a text structured around both the DNA double-helix and Bach's *The Goldberg Variations*, a combination befitting an essay focusing on these novelists' shared interest in systems novels, in science and information theory, and in prodigality writ large (prodigal: "given to reckless extravagance") (16). But Wallace's fame, particularly since his 2008 suicide, has somewhat cut him free from the contemporaries with which he was originally associated. The time is right, then, to revisit this flawed but in many ways astonishing, and astonishingly prophetic, novel and tease out exactly how Powers, in anticipation of Wallace, suggests we move beyond postmodern irony and toward a fiction of pragmatic engagement with readers and the outside world.

Wallace's critique of postmodern irony can be sourced back to Søren Kierkegaard's critique of same. Allard den Dulk, the most recent critic to examine the Kierkegaardian roots of Wallace's critique, even quotes a private letter from Wallace, dated March 2006, in which Wallace declares, "I too believe that most of the problems of what might be called 'the tyranny of irony' in today's West can be explained almost perfectly in terms of Kierkegaard's distinction between the aesthetic and the ethical life" (den Dulk, 59n). Den Dulk goes on to explain that, in Kierkegaard and in Wallace, "irony is not just a verbal strategy, an indirect or ambiguous way of expressing oneself, but an *attitude toward existence*" (46). Although Wallace accepts that an ironic attitude can liberate the individual from the crass hypocrisy of contemporary existence, it can do little more than that. As Wallace famously observes in "E Unibus Pluram," irony "serves an almost exclusively negative function. It's critical and destructive, a ground-clearing. Surely this is the way our postmodern fathers saw it. But irony's singularly unuseful when it comes to constructing anything to replace the hypocrisies it debunks" (*Supposedly* 67). Or, as den Dulk argues, Wallace targets "an automated, total irony that is no longer a means to overthrow hypocritical, unquestioned truths, but rather an instrument of cynicism that makes it incredibly difficult for individuals to realize a meaningful life" (47). Wallace's critique, then, although it is grounded in a historical trajectory, is also existential, a private experience for which he provides a private, individualized cure: move past irony and, in den Dulk's formulation, "*choose* to attend to something. Thereby, we commit ourselves to the world and start taking up our task of self-becoming" (58).

Like Wallace, Powers accepts, and also finds problematic, the fact that irony is the primary mode for thoughtful people confronting the hollow simulacrum that is contemporary existence. Rachel Hobson, *Prisoner's Dilemma*'s top ironist, declares that, because "she was condemned to a culture that mandated magnets on the refrigerator, she would be a blessed saint of refrigerator magnets. She lived in a land where folks in thirty-second spots on national TV made love to their clothes because they'd been washed in the right sauce. So be it: she'd prewash and fabric-soft with the best of them" (61). Artie describes irony's ascendency as "the antieverything infection" (170). But for Powers, irony also becomes the only way to confront a world that has become accustomed to mass genocide, nuclear brinkmanship, and environmental devastation. At one point Artie asks himself, "Why was it so impossible, these days, to experience anything, to look out the window and *feel*?" and just as quickly provides an answer: "Because the question itself was already self-conscious. Because the basic four-chambered heart and the standard two-chambered brain were not designed to live in the kind of place they had made of the world" (170). Unlike Wallace, however, Powers does not propose that we escape irony, but rather that we reappropriate it for positive means, and here is where his work dovetails with that of Rorty. Deliberately or not, Powers engages productively with all three terms in Rorty's title. At the novel's center lies Eddie Hobson, who has spent his fatherhood quizzing his children on history and challenging them with riddles and paradoxes. These games are designed to help his children understand what Rorty calls their "historical contingency," as opposed to their metaphysical essence, which latter concept Rorty dismisses as a phantasm. As Rorty explains, "Our language and our culture are as much a[n historical] contingency, as much a result of thousands of small mutations finding niches (and millions of other finding no niches), as are the orchids and the anthropods" (16). Similarly, Eddie tries to show his children that "the incomprehensible climax of the present" is the sum total of all the countless "justifiable injustice[s]" that have preceded us (243). As he sees it, "One's only hope of salvation lay in finding out where history dropped you down" (50). In language that echoes Rorty's, Eddie understands that both his children and his former students will enter the world via "a series of small and unnoticed decisions—thousands of them a day. More often than not, these incremental decisions are made in complete ignorance of the Big Picture," that last phrase one of the novel's key terms for History writ large. (244). His lifelong project is to "see if big is the sum of little, or if the two belong to unjoinable worlds" (243).

Powers's treatment of irony in the novel, though it is complex and nuanced, also overlaps with Rorty's definition. For Rorty, an ironist isn't a mere cynic; rather, she is someone who understands that all of her most cherished beliefs and ethical engagements are also unavoidably contingent. Ironists do not hold a set of "beliefs," which they insist are "true" in some metaphysical sense; rather, they accept that they possess merely "a set of words to justify their actions, their beliefs, and their lives," which set Rorty calls a person's "final vocabulary." An ironist, in his terms, is someone who "fulfills three conditions":

(1) She has radical and continuing doubts about the final vocabulary she currently uses, because she has been impressed by

other vocabularies, vocabularies taken as final by people or books she has encountered; (2) She realizes that arguments phrased in her present vocabulary can neither underwrite nor dissolve these doubts; (3) Insofar as she philosophizes about her situation, she does not think that her vocabulary is closer to reality than others, that it is in touch with a power not herself. (73)

Rorty insists that such a stance does not lead to nihilism or empty relativism. Rather, he affirms "the fundamental premise . . . that a belief can still regulate action, can still be thought worth dying for, among people who are quite aware that this belief is caused by nothing more than contingent historical circumstance" (189). Even more importantly, an ironist, because she does not elevate her "final vocabulary" to that of metaphysical truth, is better able to identify imaginatively with others, particularly those who operate according to a different, but equally contingent, final vocabulary. Solidarity, the final term in his trio, does not emerge from a "recognition of a core self, the human essence, in all human beings"; rather, it is a product of "the ability to see more and more traditional differences (of tribe, religion, race, customs, and the like) as unimportant when compared with similarities with respect to pain and humiliation— the ability to think of people wildly different from ourselves as included in the range of 'us'" (192). In other words, recognizing historical contingency allows ironists "to extend our sense of 'we' to people whom we have previously thought of as 'they'" (192).

Powers proposes a very similar vision of ironic solidarity, one grounded not only in a recognition of one's historical contingency but also in the importance of imaginative identification and—here we have the final component that connects Powers's novel with Rorty's text—imaginative art writ large. Eddie's aim in challenging his children always to understand "where history dropped [them] down" is to turn "the We and They . . . into You and You" (50)— that is, to increase solidarity. But that solidarity is grounded always in an acknowledgment of potential futility—as Eddie repeatedly advises, "Suppose the world were already lost?"— that also extends to the novel's heightened self-awareness of its own status as text, as fiction. According to Joseph Dewey, Powers suggests that fictions are "bravura acts of the imagination in narrow retreat from the disturbing implications of the immediate" (29). But fictions can also be a way to connect with other readers and so spring us free from our imaginative prisons. Powers, drawing the term from Beirut hostage Terry Waite, calls this aspect of reading "productive solitude," with reading itself deemed "the last act of secular prayer" ("Art of Fiction" 113). Artie's key term "crackpot realism" can be read not only as Powers's Rorty-inflected means toward ironic solidarity but also as a way to break out of the insularity of traditional postmodern metafiction. "Crackpot realism," as Artie explains, "meant that he and his remaining fellow genes, if they hoped to survive [their father's] disappearance, had to will, for everything they were worth, that he not disappear" (313–14). This attitude, Artie argues, is "the only way . . . to release the us-and-us that was trapped inside the you-versus-he" (313). At the same time, the term accounts for the novel's seemingly incompatible combination of playful narrative self-awareness and urgent ethical engagement. For, as Rorty would agree, acknowledging narrative art's artificiality does not undermine its utility. Quite to the contrary, narrative art, more so than philosophy, can help us understand and identify with others for the simple fact that it provides "detailed description of what unfamiliar people are like and of redescription of what we ourselves are like" (xvi). Such descriptions and redescriptions, in Powers's terms, provide perhaps "the only and awful way back to We" (313).

The members of the Hobson family divide neatly into two camps. For all their joking around, Artie and Rachel are both bitter, their particular form of irony laced with acid, whereas Lily is a disillusioned former early-1970s activist who cannot entirely shake her former idealism, and Eddie Jr. is the novel's most hopeful and optimistic character, a heedless romantic who actively seeks "deep mischief. The kind of over-his-head treading for dear life that he lived for" (188). Similarly, Powers deliberately contrasts Eddie Sr.'s dark humor and despairing vision with Ailene's not-entirely-guileless Midwestern cheer. Although all the members are ironists in Rorty's sense, the six of them provide a wide range of possible ironic modes that can be organized into two broad categories, that of the "cynical" and the "naïve." "Crackpot realism" can thus be read as a variation on Wallace's paradoxical idea in that it is a way to hold out a "crackpot" hope for salvation while maintaining a cynical, realistic perspective on one's chances for success. But, as suggested above, "crackpot realism" might also describe Powers's fictional technique in Prisoner's Dilemma—namely, his joining of

postmodern metafiction and naïve earnestness. As Powers admitted
in his "Art of Fiction" interview in *The Paris Review*, his goal as
a writer is to "have it both ways" and "to create a kind of book
that is both realistic and metafictional" ("Art of Fiction" 125).
In this reading, Eddie Jr. stands in for the postmodern irony and
self-reflexive defeatism of the John Barth and Thomas Pynchon
generation, while the four Hobson offspring represent Powers's
more hopeful, and self-consciously "naïve," generation.

   Before they became known as "postmodern writers," Barth
and Pynchon, along with Kurt Vonnegut and Joseph Heller, were
called "black humorists," a term designed to convey these writers'
particular brand of cynical comedy or, in Barth's case, cheerful
nihilism. The first generation of writers to operate under the
heretofore unimaginable threat of man-made nuclear annihilation,
they responded to the terrifying aftermath of World War II and the
brinkmanship of the Cold War with a bitter but comedic defeatism
best defined by Heller's *Catch-22* and Vonnegut's *Slaughterhouse-
Five* but also evident in Pynchon's *V.* and Barth's early existential
comedies, *The Floating Opera* and *The End of the Road*. Eddie
Sr., a Depression-era child and World War II vet, is a member of
Heller and Vonnegut's generation. Aged thirteen in 1939 (Powers
46), he would have been born in 1926, three years after Heller
and two after Vonnegut. One character overtly describes Eddie's
particular form of irony as "black humor" (199), while Eddie Jr.
describes it "a kind of sarcasm, but not sarcastic. He jokes the way
people hug at fiftieth-year reunions: too much back-slapping, when
what everybody really wants to do is kiss all those shattered faces
and weep. He parodies everything" (199). Eddie's favorite book is
The Decameron, which Artie describes thus: "a handful of people
escape the Black Death and keep themselves alive and entertained
in their exile by telling one another fantastic stories" (327). Eddie
Jr. also explains that his father "reads everything, and then gets
talkative about it all, and drags everybody down in to the facts
with him" (199). Conversely, "the more Artie learns, the quieter he
gets" (199).

   Eddie's own form of defeated black humor can be sourced
directly to his having witnessed the first atom bomb test while
stationed in New Mexico at the end of the war. The moment Eddie
sees that blast, he realizes he no longer has "the power to make
any difference" (322). In retrospect, Eddie dates the change to six

years earlier, specifically to 1939, the year of both the New York World's Fair in Flushing Meadow, Queens, with its hopeful "World of Tomorrow" exhibit, and Hitler's invasion of Poland. Artie discovers among his father's papers a "blue-lined sheet of notebook paper" with the date "September 1, 1939," scrawled across the top containing thirteen-year-old Eddie Sr.'s explication of Rudyard Kipling's "If," which the youthful Eddie describes as his "favorite poem" and which the older, post-atomic-bomb Eddie continues to recite with bitter irony (239). That date, of course, also serves as the title of W. H. Auden's famous poem in response to Hitler's invasion, a poem that concludes,

> Yet, dotted everywhere,
> Ironic points of light
> Flash out wherever the Just
> Exchange their messages;
> May I, composed like them
> Of Eros and dust,
> Beleagured by the same
> Negation and despair,
> Show an affirming flame. (lines 91–99)

Whereas this ringing finale holds out "ironic" hope in a solidarity that will combat "negation and despair" with "an affirming flame," Eddie simultaneously reflects Auden's more defeatist observation, from "In Memory of William Butler Yeats," that "poetry makes nothing happen" (ln. 36), a line that Powers declares is "one of [his] epigraphs" ("Art of Fiction" 118). As Eddie declares elsewhere in one of his Hobstown recordings, dated "Hobstown: 1939," "The possible no longer keeps pace with the necessary. Little no longer divides into Big. Eddie Hobson no longer has anything to do with events" (46).

Eddie's mysterious disease serves as the novel's most fanciful metaphor for this terrifying disconnect between "little" and "Big." Undiagnosed for more than twenty years, the disease exhibits as a series of unexplained "fits" and, it is implied, hallucinations. When in the grip of the disease, Eddie "sees" something he refuses to describe to his family. After he finally does turn himself into the VA for testing, his physician discovers that Eddie's symptoms are identical to those of someone who has suffered from radiation poisoning. The implication is that Eddie was poisoned when he stepped outside the barracks and saw the bomb test, and that what he "sees" during his fits is a replay of that blast. But the doctor goes on to assure Artie that "the disease could not possibly drag on malignant that way, so long after exposure. Even if some of the symptoms matched, the etiology was all wrong" (326). Perhaps anticipating this diagnosis, Eddie urges Artie to seek out the work of Dr. Harold Wolff, a neurosurgeon at Cornell who hypnotized a group of experimental subjects and, touching their skins with a pencil, told them he was branding them with a red-hot iron. Afterwards many of the subjects developed blisters on their skin where the pencil had made contact. "The point is," Artie concludes, "certain inarguably physical responses needing, so we think, physical causes, can be created, if you will, by sufficiently powerful imagination" (236). Eddie's disease, then, is psychosomatic and is thus a willed attempt to connect "little" with "Big," to keep alive the one moment when he brushed up against the Big Picture. But it is also the novel's most flamboyant metaphor, for Eddie is sick with nothing less than the twentieth century itself.

Fittingly, Eddie is responsible for the novel's most overtly postmodern feature, the Hobstown narrative. Beginning in the late 1950s, in the wake of his first attack from the disease, Eddie began dictating elaborate narratives onto reel-to-reel tapes, the whole of which the Hobson children refer to as "Hobstown." The recordings are "like chunks of a dream, melting into each other, changing shape without any connection" (287). Hobstown represents an alternative world, a place where Eddie can reshape history into a useful and redemptive fiction. The world he creates with his imagination is "the only sovereign state ever to practice the principle of complete self-sufficiency: sacrifice everything, pare it away until all that's left is the unencumbered mystery of getting along with, for, and by yourself" (124). In keeping with the novel's Game Theory motif, Dewey views Hobstown as an "escapist" fiction, a means of retreat from the immediate world that paradoxically creates another prison. Its postmodern self-consciousness emerges from the novel's suggestion that "virtually any text produced by the post-Hiroshima imagination is essentially a captivity narrative" (36). The narratives mix historical events with fanciful invention, blurring the line between art and reality in the hope that if the outside world can shape his fiction, then perhaps his fiction can reconnect to the outside world. Like Eddie's disease, which inspired them, the Hobstown narratives try to show how a "sufficiently powerful imagination" can actually make a physical and palpable difference in the world. Yet Eddie's narratives also undermine this same "crackpot" hope with the grimly "realistic" acknowledgment that, as Powers observes, "In the cauldron of unresolved and unresolvable disputes between people, . . . [d]oes art do anything?" ("Art of Fiction" 118). This paradox sits at the very center of the novel's complex, multilayered narrative strategy.

One of the "stars" of Eddie's Hobstown fantasy is Bud Middleton, part of a fictional all-American family created by the Westinghouse corporation to "serve as model Americans" and to promote "the immense and undeniable benefits of Westinghouse's product, the product Bud's dad calls 'science's greatest gift to the world of the future'" (42). The Middletons are white, middle-class, and, like the Hobsons, Midwesterners. As products of US consumer culture, they are ripe for ironic ridicule. Yet despite pointing out the Middleton's ultimate purpose—namely, to sell washing machines—Powers is only partially interested in "exploding the hypocrisies" represented by the corporate-constructed Middleton family. For one thing, such a critique is already old hat. In 1988, the time of the novel's publication, the US nuclear family, as typified by the Middletons—Mr. and Mrs., Bud and his sister Babs—was already a tired object of postmodern ridicule, as evidenced by such "edgy" programs of the era as *The Simpsons* and *Married . . . with Children*, the latter of which featured a four-member family, The Bundys, who already provided a one-to-one dismantling of the Middleton ethos.

Here again, Powers predates his Midwestern colleague Wallace, who, in "E Unibus Pluram," singles out *Married . . . with Children* as an example of late 1980s television's successful process of "absorbing, homogenizing, and re-presenting the very same cynical postmodern aesthetic that was once the best alternative to the appeal of Low, over-easy, mass-marketed narrative" (*Supposedly* 52). For Wallace, the dysfunctional Bundys, with ineffectual Al at the head, typify this televisual tactic of "heaping scorn on pretentions to those old commercial virtues of authority and sincerity—thus (1) shielding the heaper of scorn from scorn and (2) congratulating the patron of scorn for rising above the mass of people who still fall for outmoded pretentions" (61). Powers's use of the Middletons, in its assumption that such scorn is already baked into the postmodern pie, moves beyond mere ridicule to some form of redemption. We move *through* our cynicism to a new appreciation of the Middletons as representative after all—but representative of various qualities that the book's readers cannot so easily elide through ironic distance.

Once reanimated into a fictional character within Eddie's narrative, Bud Middleton becomes for Powers a way back into the reality behind the World Fair's shiny surface, and a means by which Eddie and Powers can bridge "the tremendous gulf" that stretches between the Fair's constructed utopia and the "real world" that exists "just down the pastel avenue, shading into the hues of the fair's color-coded 'zones'" (43). "A creation of the same fair," Bud cannot see any of this, of course, for the simple fact that "he has just the degree of insight the fair gives him and no more" (43). Conversely, Eddie Jr., who writes letters to Bud and naively treats him as a flesh and blood friend, does "know, without knowing, that something terribly wrong infects the world of 1939" (45–46). But young Eddie represents less a contrast with guileless Bud than Bud's only slightly more attentive double. Although Ed only met the Middletons once, "in the Westinghouse film," he feels obscurely that "their future seems somehow crucial to [him]" (45). Eddie recognizes that his life is *more like the Middletons* than not, in the sense that his life in 1939 "is more benign and beneficent than ever," and *that's* just the problem. "Enjoying life like everyone else might actually make matters worse" (46). Powers's strategy here is to offer up the Middletons not to invite scorn, thereby "congratulating the patron of scorn for rising above the mass of people who still fall for outmoded pretentions," as Wallace has it, but rather to inspire self-questioning on the part of his readers. If the Fair is a model of the world, to what degree are we, like Bud, creations of that Fair, content to view our world "with just the degree of insight" that narrow world gives us "and no more"?

Throughout the Hobstown sections, Powers emphasizes how our narrow-horizoned enclosure in the present obscures the various ways our day-to-day behavior shapes the future. The novel terms this temporal myopia "The Dominant Tense" (42). "We make tomorrow's archaeology today," Eddie points out, and so Hobstown is both an historical "treasure hunt" in its careful recovery the pop-cultural and historical detritus of 1939 and an alternative history

(43). Borrowing his technique from the State Fair's Time Capsule, which attempted to include "everything we are at that moment" and send the whole mass forward into the future—specifically the year 6939—Powers takes us back to 1939 and invites us, despite our knowing how everything eventually turned out, to imagine a different 1939, one where the actions taken at the time result in a better outcome. Philip Roth, in his alternative historical novel *The Plot Against America*, contrasts "history" with the "relentless unforeseen." As Roth's narrator explains, "Turned wrong way around, the relentless unforeseen was what we schoolchildren studied as 'History,' harmless history, where everything unexpected in its own time is chronicled on the page as inevitable. The terror of the unforeseen is what the science of history hides, turning a disaster into an epic" (114). Via Hobstown, Powers both recovers "the relentless unforeseen" and rewrites the "inevitable" as possibly within our power to change.

Even this last hopeful agenda is undercut by the novel's dour realism, yet another instance of Powers combining naiveté and cynicism. The novel simultaneously suggests possible instances in which small, incremental actions can change the Big Picture while also acknowledging that, more and more, "Little no longer divides cleanly into Big" (46). The hopeful part of this equation is best typified by the Butterfly Effect, "that model of random motion describing how a butterfly flapping its wings in Peking propagates an unpredictable chain reaction of air currents, ultimately altering tomorrow's weather in Duluth" (94). Here, small divides into big. In direct contrast, Powers also invokes the "Voting Fallacy," which argues that "no matter which candidate I like, . . . *my* vote itself will not alter the outcome" (55). One of the novel's central questions, then, is "How much can one vote count?" (100). Although the cynic in us knows that "one vote" by itself cannot change the fate of millions, Powers argues that "the world is not millions; it is one and one and one" (265). Hobstown's major piece of historical revision, the fictional Disney film *You Are The War*, crystalizes how Powers hopes narrative art can, through the process of readerly empathy, build Rorty-like solidarity among the atomized "one and one and one." "How will telling my story do anything?" Eddie asks as the filming winds up, to which Disney replies, "We show them how *one* life, yours, changes all the others it touches" (266). So long as Eddie, in the film, believes that "what happens to [him] makes

[a] difference," the film's viewers will be inspired to believe the
same thing about themselves, thereby enhancing the power of each
individual vote (266).

The Dominant Tense strategy also reveals how pervasively the
bigger currents of the historical moment infect the art of any given
moment, the suggestion being that the valence can thereby be turned
around. Hobstown is constructed almost entirely around pop culture,
"escapist" art whose purpose is to insulate us from the relentless
unforeseen. Nevertheless, even the most banal pop art is connected
to the Big Picture. Powers fancifully suggests that Disney's *The
Three Little Pigs* "coincides with Hitler's appointment as German
chancellor and the establishment of the Third Reich" (98–99) and
Snow White "at last appears in the year of the *Anschluss*, the war in
Manchuria, and the Sudetenland crisis," while its story—"a heroine
poisoned by a wicked witch's apple and resurrected by a prince with
the aid of seven small allies—is construed as a thinly veiled allegory
in America's raging isolationist debate" (99). Art is not shut out
from the world; the Big Picture leaks in. Just as "reality" enters into
those "other worlds, cartoon realities synchronized to music," so,
too, does "reality" intermingle with the novel's postmodern parody,
never more so than in the relationship between Bud Middleton and
young Eddie Hobson. In Disney's original vision for *You Are the
War*, the star was to be Bud, "the force leading the way to that
promised future" (184). Disney's reasoning is sound enough, given
that Bud, as a product of the World's Fair, is associated with the
World of Tomorrow. Instead, Disney casts Eddie, whom he "snares
just in time, before [Eddie] is touched by outside developments"
(263). Eddie "enters" the novel's most elaborately fictionalized and
metafictional component, thereby creating an "opening" in this self-
reflexive structure into the "real world."

Powers clarifies his purpose in this regard via Disney's ingenious
use of color in the film. Whereas the scenes of Eddie Hobson's day-
to-day life on the home front are filmed in black and white, the
scenes in which Mickey Mouse plucks Eddie out of his world and
shows him "unsuspected connections" to the Big Picture are filmed
in "living color" (266). At one level, Powers suggests that the narrow
moral simplicity of Eddie's childhood is a "black and white" world
while the broader world of major political forces is much more
complex and layered. At the same time, Powers also dramatizes
how Eddie's remembered past is a construction inevitably shaped

by and filtered through Eddie's obsessive absorption in 1930s cinema. Eddie gets to see the Big Picture, cast in technicolor, only when his animated Virgil, Mickey Mouse, takes him there. Here Powers makes resourceful use of Disney's "Fairy Dust," which Peter Pan's Tinkerbell in subsequent Disney marketing taps from her wand to set a Disney cartoon, TV program or motion picture into action. Fairy Dust here is both the fanciful stuff that "animates" the imagination and "imagination reified"—the stuff that makes both art and nuclear bombs (214). As Scott Hermanson points out, "In startling fashion, the film's animators speak of magic fairy dust in terms eerily similar to the Manhattan Project" (69). At the film's climax, Eddie, still in his black-and-white world of "gray scales and halftones," steps outside for a cigarette, just as the real Eddie did at the end of World War II, and "is greeted in mid-turn by the glorious light of day" (312). The burst of light he sees is the blast from the test bomb. For the first time in the film, "Hobson's black-and-white surroundings go color," a moment Powers terms "the high-water mark of forties realism" (312). The self-reflexive, heavily mediated Hobstown narrative has now intersected with "reality," a reality that, the novel argues, is a made thing, created, like an animated film, by a dizzying series of tiny, incremental steps. Significantly, Eddie concludes the Hobstown narrative by having his fictional doppelgänger, still stunned by the bomb blast, register "the beating of insect wings," a clear evocation of the Butterfly Effect.

In a similar fashion, Powers interweaves the Hobstown narrative with the ostensibly "realistic" Hobson chapters. As with the color scheme devised for *You Are the War*, the two narratives also collapse any neat distinctions between the mediated and the real. One of the most persistent criticisms about Powers's work is that his dialogue is too wooden and self-conscious, part of a general complaint that his work is intellectually ambitious but emotionally stilted. In his review of Powers's 2003 novel *The Time of Our Singing*, Peter Dempsey admits, "Powers is no Elmore Leonard when it comes to dialogue," while James Wood, in his review of 2009's *Generosity*, concludes that Powers "makes beautiful connections between concepts . . . but primitive and mechanical connections between his characters" ("Face the Music"; "Brain Drain" 61). Yet it is possible that both critics draw too hard a line between Powers the technician and Powers the sentimentalist. That line is much blurrier than many of his harshest critics have acknowledged, such that the moments of sentimentality in his work are inextricable from the fiction's postmodern self-consciousness. For instance, throughout the Hobson chapters, the novel's ostensibly "realistic section," the dialogue is deliberately stylized and artificial, each line the set up for a zinger rejoinder, every possible pun exploited and punchline embraced, exactly as it would be in a half-hour family sitcom, which the Hobson chapters in part parody. In fact, Eddie Jr., in a brilliant chapter that replays the "Buffalo Gals" sequence from *It's a Wonderful Life*, argues that his family "might make a halfway decent sitcom" (189). Again, as in Hobstown, sitcoms and sentimental, pre-ironic cinema are not being employed for the purposes of ridicule but rather repurposed ironically in the hope of recovering the earnestness lurking within those mediations.[1] Eddie Jr.'s turn as a late-Seventies, teenage Jimmy Stewart succeeds as both parody and a moment of wistful charm; what a sophisticated postmodern viewer of *It's a Wonderful Life* might dismiss as too saccharine on its face gets resurrected here but in a bleak, realistic context whereby the maudlin sweetness emerges intact, and *earned*. Powers signals his purpose when he has Eddie describe his father as someone who mocks and "parodies everything" but who is "totally maudlin underneath. A sentimentalist who refuses to put himself at the mercy of caring what happens to other people" (199).

Powers links the two narrative strands via a third strand that neatly synthesizes the two and also makes clear how the novel suggests narrative can be part of a small, possibly Quixotic, but no less necessary process of solidarity building in the Rorty sense. In the final Hobstown reel, Eddie visits the A-frame house Disney inhabited during the filming of *You Are the War* and, after listening to Disney's final dictated message, tapes over it with a message of his own: "Let's start again, from scratch. Let us make a small world, a miniature of a miniature, say an even half-dozen, since we screw up anything larger. Let's model the daily workings of an unremarkable,

---

[1]Dewey makes a similar argument when he asks, "Is *Prisoner's Dilemma* then a painful realistic memoir of a troubled son and haunted family . . .? Or is this a rollicking, decidedly postmodern de/construction of the de/reconstruction of the seductive (melo)dramatic theater of hot and cold wars that uses—and parodies— both that generation's sitcom expectations of the suburban family and its embrace of escapist entertainment" and concludes, "Not surprisingly, it is something in between" (34). My argument is that it is *both*.

mid-sized family, and see if we can't get it right" (333). Following his father's disappearance from the VA, Artie breaks into the prison of his father's bedroom and locates the Hobstown reel. After the tape spools out, Artie hits "record" and begins dictating the novel's opening lines, thereby erasing his father's elaborate creation and replacing it with the string of personal memories from Artie's past that have been alternating with Hobstown throughout the novel. According to Artie, his father had "deliberately left the door open" and now it was the children's responsibility to fulfill their father's admonition to "do what you can while you can before you cannot. Having listened in, they were now each of them condemned to do something about the ending" (344). Beneath the personal narrative resides the fanciful tale that seeks to connect the little to the big, the two texts forming a palimpsest that models in miniature the larger demands of the novel to "struggle with the same entrapping question of what, if anything, one private citizen can do to make the shared scenario less horrible" (331). The "crackpot" solution is a Rorty-like attempt to build solidarity through the sharing of narrative—in other words, narratives like *Prisoner's Dilemma* that disclose the connections between the private and the public, the personal and the political, but do so not by seeking, in Rorty's words, the "human essence, in all human beings"—the novel's overt self-consciousness clearly announces its logocentric suspicions— but rather by revealing the "similarities with respect to pain and humiliation" (192).

This solution also serves as the novel's sly solution to the Game Theory problem that gives the novel its title. As Eddie Jr. understands the model, if the two prisoners reason separately, "they drag themselves down," so Eddie asks, "But what about reasoning from above?" (71). Narratives like *Prisoner's Dilemma* are one way for the prisoners—that is, all of us, trapped in our own matrices— to reason from above. Although we each experience the novel in isolation, we become, as readers, part of a larger community of people we do not know personally and will never meet. In Wallace's famous phrase, the novel gives us "imaginative access to other selves" and thus allows us to "identify with characters' pain" so that we may "more easily conceive of others identifying with our own" (*Conversations* 22). Like those prisoners who do not know how the other prisoners will act, we can only do what Dewey terms "the illogical: cooperate, even trust, and find the generosity to risk even the smallest gestures of inclusion and compassion" (48). That shared readership extends our sense of "we." And it is no accident that Powers has built his narrative from "escapist" artifacts such as Disney cartoons and Frank Capra movies and family sitcoms, because escape from our own prisons of the present, and of our cynical helplessness in the face of the shared scenario, is the qualified freedom toward which this replete and unaccountably overlooked novel points us.

The novel's affinity with Rorty also opens up an additional connection to Wallace that the subsequent pages of this volume will explore at greater depth. Although Wallace was, as far as I can tell, relatively silent on Rorty's influence on his own thinking, he tellingly titled his curious 2004 story, "Philosophy and the Mirror of Nature" (included in *Oblivion*), after Rorty's groundbreaking 1979 work of anti-epistemology. Given that Rorty's volume, also titled *Philosophy and the Mirror of Nature*, bears little to no relationship to Wallace story about spiders and plastic surgery gone wrong, Wallace appears to have chosen the title, in part, as a source clue, similar to his otherwise gratuitous naming of Jim Incandenza's film *It Was a Great Marvel That He Was in the Father without Knowing Him* after Harold Bloom's prologue to *The Anxiety of Influence*, as touched upon in the previous chapter. In both cases, Wallace is directing his readers to the texts that inform his work.

Contingency, Irony, and Solidarity in particular belongs in dialogue with Wallace's work, as concisely noted by Thomas Tracey in his essay, "The Formative Years: Wallace's Philosophical Influences and *The Broom of the System*" (see 167–69). What links the two writers is their shared enthusiasm for the work of Ludwig Wittgenstein. Wallace declared his allegiance to Wittgenstein right out of the gate, as his first novel, *The Broom of the System*, is, in many ways, an homage to, and a fictional articulation of, Wittgenstein's concept of "the language game."[2] Wallace invokes Wittgenstein's theories as a way to argue that language, while alienated from the phenomenal

---

[2]He confirmed his ongoing debt to Wittgenstein in his 1999 essay, "Authority and American Usage," wherein he not only comes down firmly as a "descriptivist" rather than a "prescriptivist" but also devotes a lengthy footnote to outlining Wittgenstein's arguments against the possibility of a "private language" (87–88 n32). For a detailed reading of *Broom*'s dialogue with Wittgenstein, see my chapter on that novel in *Understanding David Foster Wallace* (21–64).

world that, as the poststructuralists would have it, is always already deferred, also keeps us grounded in a community of other speakers. As Wallace explains, "Wittgenstein argues that for language even to be possible, it must always be a function of relationships between persons, . . . but unfortunately we're still stuck with the idea that there is this world of referents out there that we can never really join or know because we're stuck in here, in language, even if we're at least all in here together"; although we lose the world, we gain a community of speakers. This trade off Wallace has called "the single most comprehensive and beautiful argument against solipsism that's ever been made" (*Conversations* 44).

Similarly, Rorty affirms Wittgenstein's conception of language as a tool, and meaning as a function of "use," and so rejects a vision of language as a "medium" through which truths can be disclosed. The world is out there, to be sure, but truth, so called, is not. Truth, rather, is a construct of language. As Rorty puts it,

> We need to make a distinction between the claim that the world is out there and the claim that the truth is out there. To say the world is out there, that it is not our creation, is to say, with common sense, that most things in space and time are the effects of causes which do not include human mental states. To say that truth is not out there is simply to say that where there are no sentences there is no truth, that sentences are elements of human languages, and that human languages are human creations. (Rorty 5)

And because there is no way to truth—what Rorty calls "a power not ourselves"—except through language, then truths, so-called, are always contingent, that is historicized, products of human thinking. They are the accidental gifts of human history. Again, for Rorty, "Out language and our culture are as much a contingency, as much [etc] result of thousands of small mutations finding niches (and millions of others finding no niches) as are the orchids and anthropoids" of evolutionary history (Rorty 16). Such a conclusion compels Rorty to advocate for an "ironic" relationship to one's own values, which he calls one's "final vocabulary."

Wallace's paradoxical joining of "cynicism" and "naiveté" also intersects with Rorty's project. At *Infinite Jest*'s Boston Alcoholics Anonymous (AA) meetings, for instance, Wallace's narrator explains,

"It has to be the truth to really go over, here. It can't be a calculated crowd-pleaser, and it has to be the truth unslanted, unfortified. And maximally unironic. An ironist in a Boston AA meeting is a witch in church. Irony-free zone" (311). And yet AA, as Wallace describes it, consists almost entirely of clichés, the sorts of "truths" that an ironist would see through as conventional and banal. For all of that, these banal clichés work, somehow. They work despite the fact that both Wallace and the other addicts acknowledge the hackneyed hollowness of the sentiments themselves, the most important of which is the necessity of believing in a Higher Power. Midway through the novel Gately wonders, "How could some kind of Higher Power he didn't even believe in magically let him out of the cage when Gately had been a total hypocrite in even asking something he didn't believe in to let him out of a cage he had like zero hope of ever being let out of?" (468). To the question of "How AA Works," Wallace's AA veterans simply "smile their chilly smiles and say Just Fine. It just works, is all; end of story" (350). Although this valorization of "unslanted, unfortified" truth seems to refute Rorty's dismissal of same, one could just as accurately say that Wallace paradoxically affirms the ironist position via Gately's acknowledgment that he does not technically believe in the Higher Power who seems to have freed him from his cage. In other words, Wallace agrees with Rorty's argument that ironists "need to realize that a *focus imaginarius* is none the worse for being an invention rather than (as Kant thought it) a built-in feature of the human mind" or, for that matter, an actual existing transcendent entity with the power to dispense grace (Rorty 196). The same paradox holds true for Artie's crackpot realism: he must believe even if he acknowledges his belief to be based on a fiction.

In all of these cases, what matters most is what works best, a position that should not be surprising given that both Wallace and Powers draw upon the work of the most important living embodiment of the pragmatic tradition in US philosophy. In Wallace's particular case, the pragmatist strain is both deep and wide. His father, James Donald Wallace, was a moral philosopher in the pragmatist mold, while Wallace's own undergraduate honors thesis in philosophy, since published as *Fate, Time, and Language*, seeks to refute Richard Taylor's 1962 argument for fatalism on the grounds that "Taylor was offering . . . a *semantic* argument for a *metaphysical* conclusion," an approach in keeping with

Wittgenstein's famous warning, "Philosophy is a battle against the bewitchment of our intelligence by means of language" (*Fate, Time, and Language* 213; Wittgenstein 47). As I and others have shown, Wallace invoked numerous key figures from the pragmatist tradition in both his fiction and his essays. Tracey observes, "An array of references to Pragmatist philosophy are peppered throughout Wallace's . . . books," the work of William James being the most prominent (169). In the chapters that make up the current volume's second part, "The Wallace Effect," I explore how several of Wallace's contemporaries draw upon Wallace's announced debt to James's work in ways that both affirm Wallace's unique pragmatist strain and critique what they view as its, at times, homespun simplicity. While Jeffrey Eugenides is most direct in playfully poking at Wallace's Jamesean debt, Jonathan Franzen and Claire Messud also disclose a more buried but intriguing collateral dialogue between Wallace's work and that of William James's celebrated brother, the master himself, Henry.

PART TWO

The Wallace Effect

3

The Rival Lover

David Foster Wallace and the Anxiety of Influence in Jeffrey Eugenides' *The Marriage Plot*

In this volume's first half, I explored two key texts from the late 1980s that begin to articulate and put into practice a range of narrative strategies that Wallace would later telegraph as innovations characteristic of his own groundbreaking intervention into the tradition of postmodern metafiction. The purpose was to look back to the literary landscape before *Infinite Jest* in search of trace remnants of Wallace's ideas and techniques. In this section, I disclose Wallace's ghostly presence in a quartet of texts published in the wake of *Infinite Jest* and, in three of the four examples, his 2008 suicide. The first novel I address in this section—namely, Jeffrey Eugenides' 2011 novel *The Marriage Plot*—is not the earliest novel to invoke Wallace, either directly or indirectly. In fact, two of the texts addressed here precede it. Rather, I treat Eugenides' novel first because its engagement with Wallace represents the most overt and programmatic example of the four instances treated here. As such, *The Marriage Plot* provides an introduction of sorts to the key components of the Wallace Effect in its full flowering.

In *The Marriage Plot*, the character who embodies both Wallace and the Wallace Effect is the novel's romantic lead, Leonard Bankhead. Like Wallace, Leonard wears a bandana (Eugenides 45). Like Wallace, Leonard dips Skoal chewing tobacco (26). Like Wallace, Leonard is brilliant, mercurial, and depressive. Leonard even delivers various *bon mots* that Wallace first uttered in book interviews or buried in his novels. The conspicuousness of this depiction is matched by the disingenuousness of Eugenides' denials. In interview after interview, he insisted Leonard had nothing to do with Wallace. On more than one occasion, Eugenides insisted that Leonard's bandana "actually comes from Axl Rose, from Guns N' Roses," a band never mentioned in the novel, which is set in the early 1980s, before Guns N' Roses had even been formed. Still, one can understand Eugenides' impatience, particularly given the puerile, gossipy nature of so much of the speculation. Hovering about this mini-scandal was the damning charge that Eugenides lacked the imagination to create a character whole cloth. Certainly his responses seemed designed to address just such a charge. Yet he might also have been trying to forestall some of the gossip in favor of a more considered appraisal down the road. As he also pointed out to Jessica Grose in his *Slate* interview, "I'm waiting for it to pass by" (*Questions*).

Now that it *has* passed by, I wish to revisit these Wallace connections, both here and in the texts that follow, in order to account for their literary purpose. In the specific case of *The Marriage Plot*, the Wallace references are far being the product of lazy characterization; rather, they are the master key to Eugenides' novel. By invoking Wallace's presence so overtly, Eugenides transforms *The Marriage Plot* into an allegory for the contemporary post-postmodern novel and its relationship to the postmodern novels and post-structural work that preceded it. The book dramatizes a college love triangle, in which the heroine, an English major named Madeleine Hanna, wavers between two suitors, Mitchell Grammaticus, a dour, earnest religious studies major drunk on Thomas Merton and William James's *Varieties of Religious Experience*, and Bankhead himself, a science and philosophy double major who turns up unexpectedly in a semiotics class that Madeleine is also taking. Via this plot device, Eugenides stages an artistic battle between himself and Wallace that parodies Wallace's own self-conscious critiques of Harold Bloom's *The Anxiety of Influence*. *The Marriage Plot* not only revives the traditional love story by enacting a metafictional parody of same, in accordance with John Barth's strategy for postmodern fiction laid out in his 1967 essay "The Literature of Exhaustion," but also introduces a literary love triangle in which Eugenides and Wallace square off as rivals for the reader's affection.

As suggested earlier, the Wallace references extend far beyond the Skoal chewing tobacco and the bandana. Eugenides also endows Leonard with Wallace's physical bulk and courtly demeanor. "His largeness," Madeleine observes, "coupled with the softness—the delicacy, almost—of his voice, gave [her]a strange fairy-tale feeling, as if she were a princess beside a gentle giant" (45). Leonard's sexual charisma also invokes Wallace. In his Wallace biography, D. T. Max charts Wallace's extensive promiscuity, a preoccupation with sexual conquest that led him to admit that he was "'literally crazy' on the subject of sex" (Max 232). Like his character Orin Incandenza in *Infinite Jest*, Wallace's appeal to women hinged in part upon his extraordinary listening skills. As Max argues, "[H]is dedication—sexily flawed—to what might be called single-entendre connections was extremely intoxicating to some woman. For them, as several remember, he was 'like a drug'" (233). Leonard is similarly promiscuous and ostensibly other-directed. During their freshman year, Mitchell grimly watches Leonard develop a "Lothario reputation," which he hopes will "decrease his appeal," but in fact has "the opposite effect" (92). Not accidentally, one of the first times Mitchell sees "the legendary Bankhead," Leonard is "staring into a girl's face as if attempting a mind-meld" (92). Madeleine also notes that she had "never met anyone, and certainly not a guy, who was so receptive, who took everything in . . . Whenever she was with him, Leonard gave her his full attention" (61).

Leonard also speaks a very Wallace-esque language—sometimes directly. As McNally Jackson pointed out in her "Bookmongers" blog, Eugenides assigns Leonard a line of dialog drawn directly from Frank Bruni's 1996 profile of Wallace published in the *New York Times Magazine*. In the profile's opening sequence, Wallace suffers a bout of the jitters on his way to give a reading in New York and turns to a companion in his cab to ask, "Do you have my saliva? . . . Somebody took my saliva, because I don't have it" (Bruni 39). Similarly, as Leonard and Madeleine approach a lab where Leonard will finish out a year-long fellowship, Leonard asks, "Who took my saliva? . . . Do you have my saliva? Because I can't find it right now" (173). Elsewhere, Eugenides describes a photo of Leonard in which he is "standing in a snowy field, wearing a comically tall stocking cap" (92). In his author's photo for the hardcover edition of *A Supposedly Fun Thing I'll Never Do Again*, Wallace is standing in a snowy field, wearing a comically tall stocking cap.

These relatively cosmetic connections scaffold Eugenides' more substantial exploration of Wallace's sizable literary reputation. In a clever sequence, Eugenides ruefully acknowledges that contemporary literary culture now recognizes a particular literary sensibility, as well as a set of stylistic tics, as uniquely "Wallace-esque." "My goal in life is to become an adjective," Leonard vows at one point. "People would go around saying, 'That was so Bankheadian.' Or, 'A little too Bankheadian for my tastes" (57). He defines "Bankheadian" as "Of or related to Leonard Bankhead (American, born 1959), characterized by excessive introspection or worry. Gloomy, depressive. See *basket case*" (58). "Bankheadian" touches upon all the key components of Wallace's art, from its excessive subjectivity to its preoccupation with solipsism, dread, and depression. And although Eugenides has pointedly not cast Leonard as an aspiring novelist—he is, instead, a struggling biologist—Leonard continues to imagine the term "Bankheadian" in purely literary terms—or, more specifically, within the literary trajectory into which Wallace placed himself. "There's Joycean," Leonard goes on, "Shakespearean, Faulknerian," before rounding out with "Pynchonesque," "Gaddisesque," and "Nabokovian" (57). The list reads like a genealogy of Wallace's artistic forebears.

Clearly, the references to Wallace are direct and irrefutable. To understand their literary purpose, we need to start with the beginning—namely, the novel's opening sentence, which announces the book's self-conscious, literary agenda: "To start with, look at all the books" (3). The books belong to Madeleine, most of them are Victorian, and all of them are about love. Jane Austen, the Bronte sisters, Trollope, Dickens, Henry James. As she wavers between her two lovers, she works on a Senior English thesis tracing the decline of the marriage plot in the contemporary novel, this in response to a junior-year course titled "The Marriage Plot: Selected Novels of Austen, Eliot, and James," taught by an elderly professor who argued in class discussions and lectures that "the novel had reached its apogee with the marriage plot and had never recovered from its disappearance" (22). The novel thereby dismantles the convention even as it revitalizes it. More importantly, it performs this clever critique/resurrection of the "marriage plot" convention in a way that invokes Wallace's own program for the literary novel *after* postmodernism, a program built upon Wallace's own artistic battle with his great forebear, John Barth. In other words, *The Marriage Plot* invokes Wallace both in recognition of its debt to his fiction and his call for an earnest metafiction as well as in order to critique Wallace's sizable reputation and his work's reception.

As with Wallace's own work, *The Marriage Plot*'s literary self-consciousness is grounded in Barth's own "program" for the postmodern novel as spelled out in "The Literature of Exhaustion." In Barth's reading of literary history, nineteenth-century bourgeois realism gave way to modernist experimentation, a literary trajectory that transformed realism into a set of historically contingent conventions while at the same time valorizing formal innovation as a necessary component for literary art. Writers saddled with the daunting task of following the modernists—writers like John Barth, for instance—had to confront not only the "exhaustion" of realism as a mode but also the "exhaustion" of modernist experimentation itself. To overcome this apparent artistic dead end, Barth advises the artist to "turn the felt ultimacies of our time into material and means for his work—*paradoxically*, because by doing so he transcends what had appeared to be his refutation" (71). If the nineteenth-century bourgeois novel is an exhausted mode, then an ambitious novelist should write a novel that overtly demonstrates the hollow conventionality of bourgeois realism. In the end, the writer will have produced a technically up-to-date piece of self-reflexive "bourgeois realism." "This is the difference," Barth explains, "between a proper, 'naïve' novel and a deliberate imitation of a novel, or a novel imitative of other kinds of documents" (72). It *is* possible, in Barth's formulation, to execute Beethoven's Sixth Symphony today, just so long as it is "done with ironic intent by a composer quite aware of where we've been and where we are" (69).

The Marriage Plot declares its own Barthian program even in its title. Eugenides wants his readers to know that *he* knows the marriage plot is old and hackneyed and out-of-date, and yet he also wants to provide his readers with all the pleasures of an absorbing love story. He gets to do both, so long as he does so "with ironic intent," with complete and total awareness "of where we've been and where we are." Very early in the novel, Eugenides even has a character observe, "Books aren't about 'real life.' Books are about other books" (28), a formulation that neatly encapsulates the gist of Barth's argument. And yet, in one of the novel's most significant evasions, Eugenides never mentions Barth or his essay directly. Rather, Eugenides connects his metafictional strategy to the field of semiotics. Like his characters, Eugenides studied English literature at Brown between 1978 and 1983. While at Brown, he took his first course in semiotics, an experience that indelibly shaped his approach to literature. As he explained to Terry Gross, host of National Public Radio's *Fresh Air*,

> Instead of reading a text and figuring out what that text means, semiotics examines how the text gives meaning. If there's a love story, the old way of reading it would be to think about the character and the setting, and perhaps what it said about social class. Semiotics would look at a love story and compare it to all of the love stories that had been written and try to find the correspondences—the things that happened in all of those love stories—and show the artificiality of love stories. (NPR)

In many respects, this passage restates Barth's argument about the need to employ literary conventions and genres "with ironic intent" in a way that telegraphs to the reader "where we've been and where we are." The difference is that Barth is proposing a way to write, whereas semiotics lays out a way to read. So although *The Marriage Plot* does enact a metafictional parody of the traditional Victorian love triangle, it also incorporates and parodies the post-structuralist interpretive strategies that arose in concert with postmodernism writ large. There are no artists or struggling novelists in *The Marriage Plot*; there are only readers.

Two of these readers, Madeleine and Leonard, are actively reading Roland Barthes's *A Lover's Discourse*, a landmark work of semiotics in which Barthes chops up and atomizes the language of love in order to disclose its conventionality and banality while at the same time affirming it. Madeleine reads the book obsessively, and even writes a paper on it, while the omniscient narrator occasionally quotes passages from the text to offset section breaks. At one key moment in the novel, after Madeleine has said "I love you" to Leonard, he replies by opening Barthes's book to the section titled "I Love You." There Madeleine learns that, according to Barthes, "once the first avowal has been made, 'I love you' has no meaning whatsoever" (Barthes 147; Eugenides 67). For Bankhead, Barthes's text casts a cold, semiotic eye on love and de-sentimentalizes it. It functions as "a repair manual for the heart, its one tool the brain. If you used your head, if you became aware of how love was culturally constructed and began to see your symptoms as purely mental, . . . then you could liberate yourself from its tyranny" (79). For Madeleine, conversely, "the more of *A Lover's Discourse* she read, the more in love she felt" (79), largely because, for the "incurably Romantic" Madeleine, the book reads "like a diary" (87). What's more, "she recognized herself on every page . . . She didn't want to be liberated from her emotions but to have their importance confirmed" (79). In one of the novel's most telling, and significant, passages, Madeleine resolves to write her final paper in Semiotics 211 on Barthes's book, not to analyze it so much as, in her words, to "deconstruct[] Barthes's deconstruction of love" (87), a strategy that Laura Savu, in "A Difficult Dialectic: Reading the Discourses of Love in Jeffrey Eugenides' *The Marriage Plot*, identifies as Eugenides' novelistic strategy (Savu).

By jumping past Barth's metafictional program and moving directly to post-1970s literary theory as the novel's primary metafictional target—that is, by exchanging John Barth with Roland Barthes—Eugenides enacts a generational critique of Barthian postmodernism that is directly indebted to Wallace himself. Madeleine's description of her paper as a "deconstruct[ion] of Barthes' deconstruction of love" (87) invokes Wallace's metafictional parody of Barthian metafiction in "Westward the Course of Empire Takes Its Way" (see Chapter 1). What's more, Madeleine also implicitly rejects Barthes's argument for authorial absence laid out in "The Death of the Author," and she does so in a way that also invokes Wallace. Her classmates, the narrator observes, "wanted to demote the author: They wanted a *book*, that hard-won, transcendent thing, to be a *text*, contingent, indeterminate, and open for suggestions. They wanted the reader to be the main thing" (42). Conversely, Madeleine "wasn't all that interested, as a reader, in the reader. She was still partial to that increasingly eclipsed entity: the writer" (42).

In other words, she wants her reading experience to be a "living transaction between humans"—that is, reader and implied author, just as Wallace proposes.

But, of course, *The Marriage Plot* isn't merely derivative of Wallace and his arguments about the function of metafiction and his hopes for a post-ironic return to sentiment and reader–writer interaction. Rather, the novel enacts a Bloomian battle of influence with Wallace that directly parodies Wallace's own battle with Barth. The novel's one direct reference to Bloom comes via a lengthy quotation from Sandra Gilbert and Susan Gubar's *Madwoman in the Attic*, which reads, in part, "In recent years, . . . while male writers seem increasingly to have felt exhausted by the need for revisionism which Bloom's theory of the 'anxiety of influence' accurately describes, women writers have seen themselves as pioneers in a creativity so intense that their male counterparts have probably not experienced its analog since the Renaissance, or at least since the Romantic era" (Gilbert and Gubar 50; qtd. in Eugenides 178). By framing his own Bloomian battle in the context of nineteenth-century women's writing and, just as importantly, early 1980s feminist scholarship, Eugenides can swerve from the patriarchal sexism of Bloom's theory while retaining its valence. Even more importantly, Eugenides transforms Bloom's Oedipal battle between fathers and sons (or Strong Poets and Ephebes) into a love triangle. Thus does Eugenides account for the fact that the source of his anxiety is not an artistic father but rather a contemporary. Leonard and Mitchell square off for Madeleine's affection in a manner that, given the novel's self-conscious appropriation of the "marriage plot" tradition, doubles as a playful depiction of Eugenides' own artistic "competition" with Wallace for artistic preeminence.

According to this interpretation, Mitchell, Leonard's rival, must function as a stand-in for Eugenides himself—and so appears to be the case. Like his creator, Mitchell is the son of Greek immigrants. Also like his creator, Mitchell grew up in Grosse Point, Michigan, a suburb of Detroit. Mitchell's Latinized Greek surname translates loosely as "One skilled at letters." Also in keeping with Bloom's theory, Eugenides depicts Mitchell's rivalry with Leonard as a mixture of envy and resentment, both emotions springing from the fact that Madeleine chooses Leonard first. To complete this triangle, Madeline serves as both the love object and a figure for the reader-as-lover that Wallace imagines in "Westward the Course of Empire

Takes Its Way." More specifically, she serves as the ideal reader that
Eugenides and Wallace both have in mind for their brand of self-
reflective, emotive, and reader-directed work.

Although her name (particularly its spelling) invokes Proust,
specifically the "petite madeleine" that, when dipped into a cup
of tea, catalyzes his narrator's memory and launches the great
labor that will produce *A la recherché du temps perdu*, Eugenides
associates her directly with nineteenth-century heroines, particularly
female heroines in marriage-plot novels. She is, in Leonard's terms,
"a ministering Victorian angel" (354). Madeleine archly rejects the
trendy "Celestial Seasonings" with their "quotations from Lao Tzu
on the package" and remains a firm "Fortnum & Mason's drinker,
her favorite blend Earl Gray," even going so far as brewing "loose
leaves" and "using a strainer and tea cozy" (72). We also learn
that her "bedspread and cashmere sham were the same serious
shade of charcoal gray as her V-neck sweaters" (72). Typically,
Eugenides is overtly self-conscious in this characterization such
that Madeleine less resembles a nineteenth-century heroine than
represents a Victorian heroine. For instance, when, in response to
an embarrassing exchange in class, she feels "blood beating in her
ears," the narrator observes, "People blushed in nineteenth-century
novels but never in contemporary Austrian ones" (27). And when
she feels herself falling in love with Leonard, the narrator, as filtered
through Madeliene's consciousness, explains that "there were all
kinds of outmoded, novelistic words to describe how she was feeling,
words like *aflutter*" (52). Eugenides rounds out this self-conscious
portrait of a modern-day Victorian fictional character by having
Madeleine choose to enter graduate school so that she can become
a contemporary scholar of Victorian literature in the Gilbert and
Gubar mode—that is, the kind of scholars who "were talking about
all the old books she loved but in new ways" and who wrote papers
titled "Masturbation in Victorian Literature" and "The Prison of
Womanhood" and yet called Austen "the divine Jane" (177). In
short, she would become a "Victorianist" (179), a term that conveys
Madeliene's dual status as a woman who can simultaneously feel
"aflutter" and recognize the word as an outmoded semiotic sign
from a tired old discourse.

Madeleine's paradoxical ability to be both self-conscious and
naively earnest fulfills one of Wallace's most famous directives
for the post-postmodern novel—namely, that it shatter "the

delusion that cynicism and naïveté are mutually exclusive" ("E Unibus Pluram" 63).[1] Like Wallace and Eugenides, Madeleine begins both her romantic life as well as her serious literary labor in an era of postmodern irony and critical self-consciousness. The narrator observes that her "love troubles had begun at a time when the French theory she was reading deconstructed the very notion of love" (19). For all of that, she remains a hopeless romantic. As such, she neatly combines Leonard's fierce intellectualism and Mitchell's earnest, ethical directness. She can cynically recognize that all of her romantic symptoms are banal conventions while simultaneously wallowing in them like a lovesick schoolgirl. She can feel "aflutter" even while bracketing the word in scare quotes.

She is also the only character in the novel who reads fiction both cynically and naïvely, both critically and innocently. She chooses her English major "for the purest and dullest reasons: because she loved to read" (20). Before taking Semiotics 211, she lacked a "firm critical methodology to apply to what she read. Instead she had a fuzzy, unsystematic way of talking about books" (24). Semiotics 211 provides her with a "firm critical methodology" but without destroying her love of reading. She is, in other words, the ideal reader for the kind of cynical and naïve post-postmodern art that Wallace describes in "E Unibus Pluram" and which both he and Eugenides actually produce. In casting Madeleine into this allegorical role, Eugenides might also be calling attention to Wallace's own tendency, in his *Infinite* Jest–era interviews, to feminize his reader. Clare Hayes-Brady points out that "Wallace's references to his imagined readers always—to the point of affectation—envisaged the reader as female" (133). She goes on to quote the following passage from Wallace's interview with Larry McCaffery: "All the attention and engagement and work you need to get from the reader can't be for your benefit. It's got to be for hers" (*Conversations* 50).

Brilliant, charismatic Leonard wins this devoted reader's affections almost without trying. Madeleine simply cannot resist

---

[1]For a more detailed analysis of these two terms and their importance in Wallace's work, see this work's "Introduction" as well as my volume *Understanding David Foster Wallace* (16–18).

him and falls for him right from the beginning. Unfortunately for her, he proves to be a difficult lover, prone to bullying, depression, and manic episodes. Nevertheless, Madeleine's initial preference for Leonard acknowledges Wallace's preeminence in the literary landscape, while Leonard's charisma and sexual magnetism hint at the cult-like nature of current-day Wallace fandom. Conversely, dour dogged Mitchell has no path to Madeleine except by unseating Leonard. In keeping with the Bloomian model, Leonard is in Mitchell's way. Leonard got there first, and so Mitchell must wrestle with the burden of his own belatedness. Mitchell's resentment of Leonard and his efforts to overcome him as Madeleine's lover both parallel the novel's more subtle criticisms of Wallace's work and its critical reception. Their romantic rivalry opens up a dialogic space for Eugenides to stage a subtle critique—or, following Bloom, misprision—of Wallace's work and its reception that corresponds with Bloom's "revisionary ratios," in this case *Kenosis*, which Bloom defines as a "breaking-device similar to the defense mechanism our psyches employ against repetition compulsion" (14).

The first component of Wallace's work that Eugenides addresses is its preoccupation with suicide. He unveils his critique in an early scene depicting a classroom discussion of Peter Handke's *A Sorrow beyond Dreams*, a fictional memoir in which the author addresses his mother's suicide. A class member named Thurston argues that Handke "felt the weight" of the German *Sturm-und-Drang* tradition in general, and of Goethe's *The Sorrows of Young Werther* in particular, and so approached his writing not as an act of therapy but as a Bloomian battle of influence. Leonard is scandalized by Thurston's decision to treat "suicide [as] a trope" (27) and argues, "If I was going to write about my mother's suicide, I don't think I'd be too concerned about being experimental" (27). Here Leonard obliquely addresses one of the more vexing issues surrounding Wallace's posthumous reputation—namely, the ease with which the numerous suicides depicted in Wallace's work can be conflated with Wallace's own suicide. In the former case, suicide is a semiotic trope in a supremely experimental body of literary fiction; in the latter case, we have a suicide that is as real as that of Handke's mother. By having Thurston invoke *The Sorrows of Young Werther* in the context of Handke's memoir, Eugenides not only doubles back to Roland Barthes—*The Sorrows of Young Werther* is one of the most prominent source texts in *A Lover's Discourse*[2]—but also demonstrates how disturbingly easy it is to blur fact and fiction on this score. For instance, Leonard's objection to Thurston's reading—that is, his resistance to treating "suicide as a trope" in an account of an actual, rather than fictional, suicide—might apply to Steven Moore who, in the second volume of his massive encyclopedic scholarly overview, *The Novel: An Alternative History, 1600–1800*, similarly conflates the fictional Werther with an actual person, in this case David Foster Wallace himself. Moore conceives of Goethe's suicidal hero not as a young man of powerful feelings and emotions—that is, as the representative figure of the *Sturm-und-Drang* school—but rather as "a character type fairly new to fiction: someone who is smart, cultured, and sensitive, but also depressed, damaged, and self-destructive" (105)—a "character-type" that would certainly include Leonard Bankhead. Moore goes on to argue, "Like Hamlet, Werther recognizes the time is out of joint, but lacks the capacity to set it right; he more closely resembles David Foster Wallace, whose intellectual powers were not enough to overcome neurological malfunctioning" (105). In a Wallace-esque footnote, Moore directs readers to a section in Max's biography where we learn that, at one point in his twenties, Wallace, while pining after the married memoirist Mary Karr, went around calling himself "Sorrowful Werther" (Max 147).[3]

The Marriage Plot similarly critiques Wallace's depiction of depression and its link to addiction, another key trope in Wallace's work that has become unfortunately tangled with the details of

---

[2]Not accidentally, Madeleine and Leonard fall in love while reading Barthes's piece-by-piece dismantling of Goethe's novel, which itself dramatizes a love triangle similar to the one Eugenides depicts, with the key difference that the brooding, depressive, but also brilliant and charismatic Leonard marries his Lotte, thereby casting the plodding, bourgeois Mitchell as this novel's Albert.

[3]Moore was one of Wallace's most important early supporters, particularly in his capacity as managing editor for *The Review of Contemporary Fiction*, which published a special issue devoted to Wallace three years before the publication of *Infinite Jest*, an issue that featured the first print appearance of "E Unibus Pluram" and Wallace's interview with Larry McCaffery, two documents that have so firmly shaped the critical approach to Wallace's fiction that Adam Kelly refers to both texts as the "essay-interview nexus" (Kelly 4).

Wallace's own life. For Wallace's characters, depression is primarily an existential phenomenon. In *Infinite Jest*, for instance, he links depression per se to "anhedonia," defined as the "inability to feel pleasure." Anhedonia in turn is an unavoidable by-product of a contemporary postmodern culture grounded in irony, "hip cynicism," endless choice and the consciousness-escaping crutch of drugs and alcohol, the latter of which Wallace often collects under the umbrella term "Substances." Wallace also connects anhedonia and depression directly back to the *Sturm-und-Drang* Romanticism associated with *Werther*. As his hero Hal Incandenza theorizes, "It's of some interest that the lively arts of the millennial U.S.A. treat anhedonia and internal emptiness as hip and cool. It's maybe the vestiges of the Romantic glorification of *Weltschmerz*, which means world-weariness or hip ennui" (*IJ* 694). His characters struggle heroically to free themselves of drug dependency and hence depression itself, and those characters who succeed—particularly Don Gately—he casts as spiritual heroes who confront the dread of existence directly, without a safety net.

Conversely, Eugenides depicts Leonard's manic depression as a purely chemical phenomenon managed by mood stabilizers and antidepressants. Whenever Leonard does wean himself from the drugs, he inaugurates a manic episode, one of which lands him in a psychiatric hospital that, in its group therapy sessions and its cast of broken losers, deftly parodies the Ennet House and AA scenes from *Infinite Jest*. At one point, Leonard realizes "something crucial about depression. The smarter you were, the *worse* it was" (254), a line that directly echoes the narrator of *Infinite Jest*'s similar realization that "it is statistically easier for low-IQ people to kick an addiction than it is for high-IQ people" (203). In another obvious nod to *Infinite Jest* and its vast store of pharmacological detail, Leonard obsessively researches all the chemical properties of the drugs he is prescribed in an effort to master them. Yet, again, Eugenides depicts Leonard's various attempts to wean himself from his drugs not as acts of heroism but rather as the source of his trouble. Drugs in *The Marriage Plot* are not the problem: they're the solution. In a gesture that could be read as particularly damning in light of Wallace's final, tragic attempt to stop taking the antidepressant drug Nardil—an attempt that resulted in a resumption of his depression, which in turn no doubt hastened his suicide—Eugenides titles the section detailing Leonard's own final, and nearly fatal, attempt to go drug free as "Brilliant Move" (229).

But Eugenides' most compelling and discursive critique—or, again following Bloom, misprision—of Wallace's work comes to us via Mitchell himself. Whereas Mitchell's surname invokes authorship directly, Leonard's surname suggests that he perhaps puts too much value on the quality of his mind, and to his detriment, much the same way that Wallace's addicts are "also addicted to their own thinking, meaning they have a compulsive and unhealthy relations with their own thinking" (203), which is a problem given that, in *Infinite Jest*'s existentialist diagnosis, "the Disease makes its command headquarters in the head" (272). Still, Mitchell is not a writer; rather, he's a spiritual striver, a devotee of William James and Thomas Merton who, after reading these two worthies (James in particular), understands "the centrality of religion in human history and, more important, of the fact that religious feeling didn't arise from going to church or reading the Bible but from the most private interior experiences, either of great joy or staggering pain" (93). Mitchell thus functions as both Leonard's rival and his spiritual corrective; against Leonard's purely biological sense of self—and self-destruction—Mitchell affirms the importance of the soul and the spirit as the repository for our most important feelings.

Mitchell provides an additional means by which Eugenides can interrogate Wallace's own indebtedness to James's work, an intertextual nexus that numerous recent Wallace critics, including David Evans and myself, have begun tracing in earnest.[4] Once again, Eugenides introduces this Wallace echo both to pay homage

---

[4]For instance, in "'The Chains of Not Choosing': Free Will and Faith in William James and David Foster Wallace," David Evans carefully traces out James's influence on Wallace's depiction of AA as well as his diagnosis for the dread produced by the excess empty abundance of twenty-first-century postmodern culture. Evans also demonstrates how, "like James, Wallace struggled with the possibilities of faith in a fundamentally secular world" (183). Similarly, in "Trickle-Down Citizenship: Taxes and Civic Responsibility in David Foster Wallace's *The Pale King*," I analyze Wallace's allusions to James's *The Varieties of Religious Experience* and "The Moral Equivalent of War" in Wallace's final, unfinished novel, concluding that one character's "conversion [from '70s stoner] to IRS agent is a Jamesian religious conversion to an entity—which Wallace refers to throughout the novel as 'The Service'—that fulfills James's call, in ['The Moral Equivalent of War'], for a reification of martial virtues minus the bloodshed of actual war, values he outlines as 'intrepidity, contempt of

and to level a critique, the latter of which emerges late in the novel, when Mitchell undertakes a pilgrimage to Calcutta to volunteer for Mother Teresa. Eugenides places the account of Mitchell's darkest moment on this trip immediately after the account of Leonard's "Ennet House"–like recovery from his last manic episode, the juxtaposition highlighting the relative superficiality of Leonard's suffering as compared to the brutal, physical suffering and unimaginable poverty Mitchell experiences in Calcutta. It is in Calcutta where Mitchell also acknowledges that his own intellectual embrace of James's unthreatening, pragmatic concept of free-floating faith might not be enough. He realizes that the "bodies at the Home for Dying Destitutes, broken, diseased, were the bodies of Christ, divinity immanent in each one. What you were supposed to do here was to take this scripture literally. To believe it strongly and earnestly enough that, by some alchemy of the soul, it happened: you looked into a dying person's eyes and saw Christ looking back" (306). This is more than Mitchell can manage, and it certainly wasn't what he thought was required of him after reading James, for whom the "literal" truth of a religious idea or experience is less important than "the inner experiences of great-souled persons wrestling with the crises of their fate" (*Varieties* 5).

Mitchell's subtle critique of James can also apply to Wallace's adaptation of James's pragmatic approach to religious faith. For Wallace's addicts, AA requires a major commitment; for Wallace's readers, AA can be too readily seized upon as a mere metaphor for an undemanding, self-congratulatory approach to religious engagement. This charge is particularly applicable to the popular response to Wallace's Kenyon Commencement Speech, which might very well be the most widely read thing Wallace ever wrote. Evans distills the speech's Jamesian strain and reads the work ultimately as "an extended paean to the importance of choice" (181). Nevertheless, that speech has long since been decoupled from Wallace's dark, complex fictional oeuvre and defanged into a piece of postmodern self-help, as confirmed by the hardbound edition published in 2010 as *This Is Water*. With

---

softness, surrender of private interest, obedience to command'" (James, "Moral Equivalent" 668; qtd. in Boswell 223–24).

its sentence-per-page design and portable–New Testament size, the book resembles nothing so much as a slick update on Kahlil Gibran's *The Prophet*. It certainly makes for a perfect graduation present. For its legions of readers, Wallace's popular address provides a cure for solipsism and alienation and our annoyance with supermarket cashier lines, and yet the fact remains that *This Is Water* diagnoses remarkably luxurious discomforts. A visit to a Kroger or an A&P grocery store after work is hardly a day at the Home for Dying Destitutes.

In keeping with the novel's love-triangle twist on Bloom's father/son scenario, the point-by-point directness of Eugenides' critique of Wallace parallels Mitchell's laser focus on Leonard as his romantic rival. In both instances, this singular focus discloses a curious blend of resentment and covert affection. Here Eugenides appears to be invoking one more work of feminist scholarship from the novel's historical present—namely, Eve Sedgwick's *Between Men*. Building on René Girard's assertion that, "in any erotic rivalry, the bond that links the two rivals is as intense and potent as the bond that links either of the rivals to the beloved," Sedgewick goes on to explore the "bond between the men" in the context of historical shifts in gendered power relations (24). In her reading of such novels as *Adam Bede* and *Henry Esmond*, she locates a repeated pattern in which the two men vying for the woman's affection merely use the woman as a means by which they can express otherwise taboo homosocial/homosexual desire for each other. On several occasions, Eugenides makes overt reference to the covert sexual bond that emerges from Mitchell's and Leonard's rivalry. When Leonard first sees a photo of Madeleine with Mitchell, he "had sized up Grammiticus according to an animal scale—antler size to antler size—and given himself the clear advantage"; nevertheless, during sex he begins to picture "Grammiticus's satyr-form clambering on top of Madeleine from behind," with the result that, "for reasons Leonard couldn't fathom . . . the idea of Madeleine wantonly betraying him with Grammaticus turned Leonard on" (263). Similarly, Mitchell discovers on his trip that his best friend Larry is gay, and as he tries to come to terms with this surprising development, he begins to see his predicament in Shakespearean terms: "Larry loved Mitchell, who loved Madeleine, who loved Leonard Bankhead" (298). There's Madeleine in the middle, between all these men.

Sedgewick's work also informs what turns out to be this love triangle's climax. In anticipation of her forthcoming graduate studies at Columbia, Madeleine and Leonard travel to New York to find an apartment. Leonard, still recovering from a manic episode on their honeymoon that left him broken and defeated, feels further unmanned by the news that Madeliene's father will financially cover for the two of them.[5] "It would be normal for the husband to pay more rent," he complains. And when she replies, "If I were the man, we wouldn't even be talking about this," he shoots back, "The fact that I feel like the wife here is sort of the problem" (374). On this same trip, she and Leonard attend a party thrown by one of Madeleine's former Brown roommates at which Mitchell, back from his pilgrimage, is in attendance. The subsequent scene dramatizes one of Barthes's figures from A Lover's Discourse titled "Connivance," and defined thus: "The subject imagines himself speaking about the loved being with a rival person, and this image generates and strangely develops in him a pleasure of complicity" (65). Mitchell, who has hated Bankhead throughout the novel, finally encounters him in his broken, feminized state, and his response invokes both Sedgwick and Barthes: "[Mitchell] was beset now, troublingly, with something resembling empathy, even affection for his onetime rival" (400). Tellingly, in a direct contradiction of Barthes's figure, the two do not discuss Madeleine at all; rather, they discuss religion, Mitchell's subject. Now that Mitchell has the upper hand—the bigger antler, as it were—he "experienced what so many people had before him, the immensely satisfying embrace of Bankhead's intelligence and complete attention. Mitchell felt that, under other circumstances, he and Leonard Bankhead might have been the best of friends" (401). But the episode also announces one additional nod to Sedgwick, for Mitchell also subsequently loses

---

[5]Leonard's breakdown references the last page of Infinite Jest, which depicts Gately's feverish memory of a massive Dilaudid binge. The novel's famous (and famously unsatisfying) final words find Gately "flat on his back on the beach in the freezing sand, and it was raining out of a low sky, and the tide was way out" (IJ 981). Similarly, Leonard concludes his final drug-free manic episode "on a beach, . . . in the middle of the night. He was looking up into the starry sky when suddenly he had the feeling that he could lift off into space, if he wanted to" (400). Perhaps coincidentally, a bit earlier in the novel, Leonard leads Madeleine on an oyster-hunting expedition, during which we're told, "The tide was out, the exposed seabed glistening in the moonlight" (346).

interest in Madeleine: "She wasn't so special, maybe. She was his ideal, but an early conception of it, and he would get over it in time" (406).

Immediately following the encounter with Mitchell, Leonard leaves Madeleine and effectively disappears from the novel, leaving the field open for Mitchell. When read in the context of the novel's artistic-rivalry motif, this late development suggests that Eugenides has deliberately arranged a victory for his own sensibility over that of his more celebrated rival. But of course the ending is not as simple as that. Although Mitchell and Madeleine do finally consummate their relationship, Mitchell finds their lovemaking to be "empty"; eventually, he realizes that "Madeleine hadn't been coming to him; she'd only been leaving Bankhead" (405). In a 1980s update of Sedgwick's famous model, Mitchell becomes merely the means by which Madeleine can still deal with her lingering feelings for Bankhead. In the same way that Leonard gets feminized at the end—at one point Madeleine refers to him as her "madwoman in the attic" (304)—Mitchell becomes the passive conduit for an otherwise elusive erotic attraction. Madeleine is finally freed of her role as "prize" and assumes her new identity as active agent of her own desires.

This realization sets the stage for the novel's clever and deeply satisfying final page, which features a "proposal" that both meets and undercuts the required conclusion of a proper marriage plot. Turning again to the literary canon of bourgeois marriage novels that has served as the novel's primary scaffolding from the opening sentence forward, Mitchell asks Madeleine if she knew of a

> novel where the heroine gets married to the wrong guy and then realizes it, and then the other suitor shows up, some guy who's always been in love with her, and then *they* get together, but finally the second suitor realizes that the last thing the woman needs is to get married again, that she's got more important things to do with her life? And so finally the guy doesn't propose at all, even though he still loves her? Is there any book that ends like that? (406)

Mitchell in effect makes an "anti-proposal" that also calls final attention to the novel's playful interaction with the literary tradition named in the title. Although he does not quite declare himself a fictional character in a novel, a la John Barth, he comes very close. Mitchell's final gesture grants Madeleine the kind of agency that would have been denied her in a traditional "marriage plot." Her story does not culminate in marriage and the loss of her identity; rather, it ends with her independence. No longer a "Victorian heroine," she is free now to go to Columbia where she will become a "Victorianist," that is a "resistant reader" who nevertheless maintains her love of the literature she interrogates. Like the novel that she inhabits, she will both uphold and update a patriarchal tradition.

Fittingly, the novel ends with the word "Yes." Madeleine delivers the word, not in response to a proposal, of course, but to Mitchells' follow-up question as to whether or not she thinks the plot he had just unfolded would make a satisfying ending to a marriage novel. More directly, the final word confirms that, in the end, Madeleine, rather than Leonard or Mitchell, is this novel's hero. "What is a hero?" Barthes asks at the end of section in *The Lover's Discourse* titled "Making Scenes." His answer is simple: "The one who has the last word" (209).

4

The Varieties of Irony

Claire Messud's *The Emperor's Children* and the Comedy of Redemption

In the second week following the September 11, 2001, terrorist attacks, conservative critic Roger Rosenblatt published a brief essay in *Time* magazine titled "The Age of Irony Comes to an End." "For some 30 years," Rosenblatt opines, "the folks in charge of America's intellectual life have insisted that nothing was to be believed in or taken seriously. Nothing was real" (79). The "horror" of the 9/11 attacks, he went on, put an end to all of that. "The planes that plowed into the World Trade Center and the Pentagon were real," he assures us. As a result, "people may at last be ready to say what they wholeheartedly believe" (79). Rosenblatt wasn't alone in making this argument. Graydon Carter, editor of *Vanity Fair*, prophesied, "There's going to be a seismic change. I think it's the end of the age of irony. Things that were considered fringe and frivolous are going to disappear" (Beers). Similarly, Camile Dodero, assessing the effect of 9/11 on Generation X, suggested, "Maybe we've just witnessed the end of unbridled irony. Maybe a coddled generation that bathed itself in sarcasm will get serious. Maybe we'll stop acting so jaded and start addressing the problem" (Dodero).

These arguments will have sounded familiar to readers of David Foster Wallace's 1990s work, both his nonfiction and his signature novel, *Infinite Jest*. Nearly a decade before Rosenblatt complained about a culture of ironists who, "seeing through everything, made it difficult to see anything," Wallace argued, "Irony only has emergency use . . . It's critical and destructive and ground clearing . . . But irony's singularly unuseful when it comes to constructing anything to replace the hypocrisies it debunks" (*Supposedly* 67). Wallace also shared Dodero's wistful hope that their generation might "get serious" and stop "acting so jaded." At the end of "E Unibus Pluram," and in a passage that has perhaps been made too much of by Wallace's readers, myself included, he called for a group of literary "*anti*-rebels" who might "dare somehow to back away from ironic watching, who have the childish gall actually to endorse and instantiate single-entendre principles. Who treat of plain old untrendy human troubles and emotions in US life with reverence and conviction" (*Supposedly* 81).

The journalists quoted above were hardly alone in seizing upon the 9/11 attacks as an opportunity to wipe away the jaded, frivolous culture of the 1990s, the same culture that Wallace's fictional project sought to redeem. In the weeks after the attacks, headlines reading "Nothing Will Ever Be the Same" (*Philadelphia City Paper*) and "America Savaged, Forever Changed" (*Detroit News*) were commonplace (Jarvis 77). Literature, too, was supposed to have changed. British novelist Martin Amis argued, "After a couple of hours at their desks, on September 12, 2001, all the writers on earth were reluctantly considering a change of occupation" (Amis). The 9/11 attacks certainly threatened the relevance of Wallace's own fiction. Though presented as an antidote to the 1990s culture of ironic detachment, Wallace's pre-9/11 work, like that of his contemporaries Dave Eggers and Stacey Richter, nevertheless "tended to hold politics at an ironic, skeptical remove," according to Nathan Oates, who goes on to argue that 9/11 inspired in US novelists a new and "heightened artistic interest in politics" (156–57).

Claire Messud explores these issues, and many others, in her acclaimed 2006 novel, *The Emperor's Children*. Indeed, Meghan O'Roarke titled her positive *New York Times* review of the novel

"The End of Irony" and quoted the same chorus of voices cited in this essay's opening paragraph (71). The novel casts a skeptical eye not only on these plangent hopes for a new post-9/11 seriousness but also on Wallace's own part in spearheading these hopes. Set in the elite literary milieu of Manhattan in the months leading up to, and immediately following, the 9/11 attacks, the novel focuses on four literary aspirants new to adulthood—the "children" of the title—all of whom in various ways hope to make their mark on pre-9/11 culture derided as "frivolous" by Rosenblatt and others. Through a persistent use of free indirect discourse, Messud mercilessly exposes her characters' self-delusions, hypocrisies, and hollowness, thus employing an inherently ironic literary method to reveal the emptiness of a culture grounded in irony. But Messud doesn't stop there, for she uses the exact same method to skewer the "emperor" of the tile, a political journalist in the mold of Christopher Hitchens who is the self-proclaimed representative of "truth" and "integrity," instances of Wallace's vaunted "single entendre principles," but who is revealed to be a philanderer, narcissist, and banal thinker. Neither cynicism nor earnestness survives Messud's ironic critique. The novel's depiction of her characters post 9/11 casts doubt upon the hopes of Carter and Dodero that these "children" would finally grow up and "get serious." Both the emperor and his children, to paraphrase the novel, have no clothes. With its knowing and deliberate allusions to Wallace and his work, the novel also invites us to read those "children" as the generation that Wallace diagnosed and sought to redeem.

The novel is rich in intertextual engagements. With its sustained linking of "clothes" and ideas, the novel is clearly conversant with Thomas Carlyle's *Sartor Resartus* (or "The Tailor Retailored"), in which a fictional German reviewer provides an elaborate commentary on an equally fictional philosophical volume timed *Clothes: Their Origin and Influence*. Similarly, two characters are depicted as having read, or in the process of reading, Leo Tolstoy's *War and Peace* and Robert Musil's *The Man without Qualities*, both of which stand in damning contrast to the novel's surface-obsessed milieu. But the text that gets mentioned most prominently in the early sections, and whose presence registers throughout, is Wallace's *Infinite Jest*. The same character who is seen reading, and not finishing, Tolstoy and Musil begins his self-education with *Infinite Jest*, which he also does not finish. While one could very likely write a full essay on each of the novel's numerous textual engagements, this essay focuses primarily on the Wallace intertext. At the same time, as will be shown, Messud entangles Wallace's fictional project with that of Tolstoy and Musil, all of whom are brought to bear upon the novel's critique of both postmodern, ironic detachment and the earnestness and seriousness that was alleged to have preceded the postmodern turn and which, according to Wallace and the 9/11 commentators, was supposed to return, phoenix-like, from the ashes.

Infinite Jest first appears in the eighth chapter, in the soapy hands of Frederick "Bootie" Tubb, one of the novel's four leading "children." Bootie, as he is called throughout the novel, is a chubby, hopelessly earnest college dropout who quits his studies at Oswego after he has a "revelation" that college, writ large, is a "farce" (59–60). His classmates don't care about learning for its own sake: they're just there to grub for grades and get laid. Determined to make something of himself, while also maintaining his intellectual purity and moral integrity, Bootie chooses to pursue an autodidact's self-education while still living at home with his mother, and the book that begins his self-designed curriculum is *Infinite Jest*, which, in an obvious nod to his surname, we first see him reading while soaking in the bathtub. Bootie chooses to begin with *Infinite Jest* because "he had heard a lot about [it], first from kids at Oswego whom he didn't particularly respect" and "then from people on the Net, and in particular from this book discussion group he'd sort of joined" (56). Several bloggers spoke of it "like it was the Bible or something," while one "lively female correspondent on whom Bootie had a virtual crush" deemed Wallace's novel "a definition of the zeitgeist" (57). Nevertheless, the 1,079-page novel proves to be slow going—Bootie is stuck at about "a hundred pages in"—and Bootie eventually gives up on the book before he makes it even halfway through.

Messud's richly ironic portrait of Bootie and his attempt to read *Infinite Jest* discloses her intimate understanding of both Wallace's novel and the cult that has arisen around it. Messud's decision to have Bootie read the book while soaking in the tub does more than call playful attention to his last name, for *Infinite Jest* is as permeated by an "infant" leitmotif as *Emperor's Children* is by the symbolism of children writ large. Wallace's novel is set in an alternative future in which calendar years have been replaced by corporate sponsorship;

not accidentally, the main action of the novel takes place during the Year of the Depend Adult Undergarment, suggesting that the novel's cast of drug-addled solipsists are, in effect, infants sucking at the teat of their addictions. The allegedly lethal film that gives the novel its title also taps into this motif: according to the most reliable account of the film, "the point of view was from the crib," while the camera "was fitted with a lens with something . . . called . . . an auto-wobble," thereby replicating an infant's primitive perspective (939). Bootie reading the novel *Infinite Jest* in the womb of his mother's bathtub replicates the fictional viewer's experience of watching the film *Infinite Jest*, a viewing experience which, in the novel, leads to paralysis and death. Finally, throughout the novel, Wallace associates infancy with what it means to be "really human," which condition the novel's hero, Hal Incandenza, conceptualizes as "unavoidably sentimental and naïve and goo-prone and generally pathetic," for the "really human" "is to be in some basic interior way forever infantile, some sort of not right-looking infant dragging itself anaclitically around the map, with big wet eyes and froggy-soft skin, huge skull, gooey drool" (695). Bootie is that Wallace-esque infant, a pudgy, doughy man-child who leaves a trail of trash and spilled food and human waste wherever he goes.

But the knowing Wallace references hardly stop here. After a month or so at home, Bootie strikes out for New York, where he hopes to be taken under the wing of his famous uncle Murray Thwaite, the novel's "emperor" figure. En route, he takes a brief detour to Amherst College, where he moves in with a childhood friend Donald, an Amherst undergraduate, and Donald's three slothful roommates. Wallace graduated from Amherst in 1985 with two honors theses: one was a philosophy essay on free will later published as *Fate, Time and Language*, the other a full-length novel that was his first published work of fiction, *The Broom of the System*. Messud confirms the purposefulness of the Amherst section by having Bootie's mother, who mistakenly thinks Bootie is taking classes toward a degree, assure herself that "some famous people had come out of there" (193). The living arrangement at Donald's off-campus apartment, with the four boys sprawled on couches and floors amid cereal bowls and other detritus, deliberately parallels a section of *Broom of the System* involving the Amherst apartment of a Wallace-esque undergraduate named LaVache Beadsman and his three pot-smoking friends, named Cat, Heat, and Breather

(236–53). That novel's heroine, LaVache's sister Lenore, camps out there for a brief period, much like Bootie. LaVache also shares Bootie's cynicism about college life, remarking to Lenore that "a really important part of being here is learning how to lie. 'Strategic misrepresentation,' we call it" (237). In this instance, LaVache is rationalizing away his business of writing term papers in exchange for drugs—an "occupation" Wallace would later assign to his character "David Wallace" in his posthumous novel, *The Pale King*.

The directness of these references encourages one to detect additional, more subtle nods to Wallace and his work. Throughout the novel, Bootie is in search of an intellectual and spiritual father. After his brief detour, he relieves Wallace of that role and presents himself as a willing disciple of his uncle, Murray, who has secretly been compiling a philosophical treatise tentatively titled *How to Live*, and which he calls his "infinitely precious file" (69, 70). The manuscript, which Bootie eventually uncovers, turns out to consist of banal platitudes and clichéd directives that at one point Murray sources back to William James's *The Varieties of Religious Experience*, a signature text for Wallace's treatment of AA in *Infinite Jest*. It is quite possible that Murray's comic foray into homespun philosophy is meant to invoke Wallace's own predilection for aphoristic directives and pragmatic life lessons, a strand of his work that culminated in his 2005 Kenyon College graduation speech, delivered a year before *The Emperor's Children*'s 2006 publication.

Like *Infinite Jest*, *The Emperor's Children* takes its title from a similarly titled work within the work, in Messud's case a trite piece of pop cultural criticism tracing the history of children's clothes and written by Murray's beautiful pixie of a daughter, Miranda, the double dedication of which reads, "For my parents, who taught me everything; and for [her husband] Ludociv, who taught me more" (315). Murray, scorned to have been usurped by his daughter's spouse, regards the dedication as evidence of "his daughter's sentimental impulses" as well as her "sloppiness," noting that the dedication in effect amounts to her saying she has learned "Everything and more," which idea "makes no sense at all" (315). *Everything and More* is the title of Wallace's 2003 "Compact History of Infinity."

These echoes are not just clever: they're also slyly critical. The critique is informed and complexly layered and, in the end, is less about Wallace than about what Wallace has come to represent for his generation. One clue as to Messud's larger agenda might be found on her own dedication page, which reads, "For Livia and Lucian, who changed everything; And, as ever, for J.W." Livia and Lucian are her children, and J. W. is her husband, the critic James Wood. Although he would strategically temper his views somewhat after Wallace's 2008 suicide, Wood was nevertheless one of Wallace's most prominent and vocal detractors.[1] Over the course of dozens of book reviews and long-form essays, Wood articulated a clear, if also relatively narrow, novelistic aesthetic that he applied consistently to his personal assessment of the many works of fiction he analyzed and reviewed, an aesthetic he formalized in his 2008 volume, *How Fiction Works*. In a eulogy to Wallace, Wood observed that "an untruthful reviewer" of the latter text "claimed that David Foster Wallace was its 'aesthetic villain'"; Wood then insists, "That is not true" ("Remembering David Foster Wallace"). True or not, the reviewer did correctly intuit that Wood's often harsh assessment of Wallace's work hinged upon the work's failure to fulfill various novelistic contracts that Wood elsewhere held up as nearly imperative. Conversely, Messud's novel seamlessly exemplifies, both in its subject matter and in its form, the kind of novelistic contract for which Wood advocates in both *How Fiction Works* and its predecessor, *The Irresponsible Self*. It is reasonable, then, to consider Wood's arguments about novelistic discourse and his critiques of Wallace's work in the context of Messud's novelistic engagement with Wallace writ large.

For several reasons, *The Irresponsible Self* bears most directly on Messud's critique of Wallace: first, because the book's introduction lays out a remarkably pertinent description of the sort of multifaceted, tolerant irony Messud employs throughout *Emperors Children* and, second, because the volume includes the essay "Hysterical Fictions," wherein Wood makes his most passionate case against the sort of fiction Wallace produces. In that introduction, Wood distinguishes between what he discerns as two distinct brands of novelistic humor, the religiously grounded "comedy of correction," which aims to "see through the weakness

---

[1] Stephen J. Burn, while visiting Wallace's home in Bloomington, Illinois, discovered that Wood sent Wallace an uncorrected galley proof of his first volume, *The Broken Estate*, which Wallace annotated. See http://www.baas.ac.uk/sjbfounders2015/.

of mankind," and the more modern "tragicomic stoicism," which Wood deems "the comedy of forgiveness," and which aims less at finding fault and more at comprehending what Wood calls "the irresponsible self" (7). Under the rubric of the "comedy of correction," Wood includes such works as Aristophanes' *The Clouds* and *The Wasps*, Erasmus's *The Praise of Folly*, Cervantes' *Don Quixote*, and, more recently, Flaubert's *Madame Bovary*, the latter of which retains "the old religious impulse to scourge and check" the book's main characters. The "comedy of forgiveness" essentially begins for Wood with Austen and continues through the work of Chekhov, Tolstoy, Bellow, and Nabokov, among many others. "If religious comedy is punishment for those who deserve it," he explains, "secular comedy is forgiveness for those who don't" (8). What's more, the "comedy of forgiveness" exchanges broad social satire for the more nuanced exploration of the interior self, where a character's self-delusions can generate both sympathy and criticism, and where "unreliability" itself can be "unreliable" and unstable, leaving readers suspended in an evaluative ambiguity that is the very ground for empathy. Characters in works grounded in the comedy of forgiveness, such as Austen's great heroines, "exercise their consciousness" and so "belong to the newer world of the novel and not of the theater," where they "are not mocked but gradually comprehended and forgiven" (14).

Deliberately or not, Wood seems here to be describing the complex ethical aims of Messud's novel. One short term that crystalizes what Wood is painstakingly atomizing is free indirect discourse, whereby a third-person narrator presents the interior thoughts of the focalized characters such that the diction reflects that of the character. Such a style produces what J. A. Culdoon identifies as a "fruitful ambiguity," which is "created when the author's hand in [a] passage is not clearly marked out from the voice of the character" (331). Messud employs this method throughout the novel, each chapter of which is focalized through one of the novel's five main characters, with Messud's effaced narrator floating above it all and listening in to each character's private thoughts, a method that holds each character up for ridicule even as it elicits our empathy. In short, the method is inherently ironic, in that each interior monologue combines direct reportage and distanced framing.

Many of the novel's reviewers took note of Messud's particular skill at managing this technique. *Bookforum* observed, "Stepping elegantly through the varieties of irony, Messud lifts superficially superficial characters out of the trivial," while several other critics compared Messud to various masters of the free-indirect style, including Jane Austen (*The Boston Globe*), Edith Wharton (*Vogue*), and Henry James (Oates 158). Other readers found the book's layered ambiguities at odds with its 9/11 setting, most prominently Arin Keeble, who confuses Messud's "comedy of forgiveness" with a "strong satirical element" that disappointingly (for Keeble, anyway) results not in a "correction" but rather in "a subliminal or unconscious restoration of equilibrium" (366, 356). Of course, Wood would say that Keeble has missed the point (and I would agree), and yet even Keeble's disapproval affirms the provocative instability of Messud's approach. In *The Art of the Novel*, Milan Kundera—whom Wood deems "much more an antique comedian than a modern one, for all the Prague sex games"—argues this brand of novelistic irony "irritates. Not because it mocks or attacks but because it denies us our certainties by unmasking the world as ambiguity"; Kundera goes onto affirm that the novel is, "by definition, the ironic art" (134).

It should not be particularly surprising that a critic and a writer who values the ambiguous potential of novelistic irony would be at odds with David Foster Wallace, whose work has consistently been read as a reaction against irony and, according to Adam Kelly, the signature corpus exemplifying "The New Sincerity in American Fiction." But the situation is more complex, and interesting and fruitful, than that. Messud's playful interaction with Wallace and Wallace's reputation consists of a gentle riposte both to Wallace's lauded critique of postmodern irony and to the antagonistic relationship he has set up between Generation X and the baby boomers, a battle that serves as the ground situation for his own intervention into the postmodernist literary tradition.

In light of the near seamless way in which *The Emperor's Children* affirms the "tragicomedy of forgiveness" that Wood extolls in his introduction to *The Irresponsibile Self: On Laughter and the Novel*, it makes sense to examine Messud's playful parody of Wallace's thinking in the context of Wood's assessment of Wallace's art and that of his peers and acolytes. As laid out in the introduction to this volume and elsewhere, Wallace's work has largely been identified as representing some "next step in fiction" (Birkerts), an advance grounded on what A. O. Scott terms "meta-irony," or what I have been calling a paradoxical blend of cynicism and naiveté. And, as has already been pointed out, literary scholars remain undecided on whether or not this advance represents a stand-alone movement, or a third-wave of modernism, or merely a sophisticated buffering of the postmodernism of old. Hence the confusing range of generic definitions assigned to Wallace's work, from Kelly's "New Sincerity" to the awkward (but serviceable) "post-postmodern." In his 2000 review of Zadie Smith's *White Teeth*, Wood proposes yet another generic definition: "Hysterical Realism."

What distinguishes Wood's attempt from that of others, aside from its searing negative take on the movement so-called, is its focus on form as opposed to tone. In his exactly contemporaneous overview of Wallace' career to date, A. O. Scott focuses primarily on the paradoxical way that Wallace's art manages to be both "unassailably sophisticated and doggedly down to earth" (40). This debate about Wallace's ability to be simultaneously self-conscious and earnest has preoccupied and bewitched Wallace's scholars almost from the beginning. Wood refuses to be thus enchanted. Carefully side-stepping the entire issue of irony, Wood characterizes the "contemporary, 'big, ambitious novel'" as a "perpetual-motion machine that appears to have been embarrassed into velocity" (178). Rather than trace the literary trajectory of these novels back to the postmodernist fiction of Pynchon, Barth, and Nabokov and then continue through the tradition to take on DeLillo, Amis, and so on, Wood confines all contemporary practitioners of the "perpetual-motion-machine" mode, from DeLillo and Pynchon to Wallace and Smith, to one big genre. While these works share a variety of "familial resemblances," he describes them all as parented by one writer: Charles Dickens. In these works, in which "stories and substories sprout on every page," the "conventions of realism are not being abolished but, on the contrary, exhausted, overworked" (179). He faults the works on this account because they seem "evasive of reality while borrowing from realism itself" (179). What's more, this "excess of storytelling" conceals a lack: "That lack is human" (182). While the characters in these novels "have a showy livelihood, a theatricality," this showiness does not hide the fact that "they are without life" (182). The novels remind him of Dickens's world, which he describes as "populated by vital simplicities" (185). Dickens's method of "creating and propelling theatrically alive characters offers an easy model for writers unable to, or unwilling to, create characters who are fully human" (184). In a telling passage, Wood argues that Dickens's "glittering liveliness is simply easier to copy, easier to figure out, than the recessed and deferred complexities of, say, Henry James's character-making" (185).

The "say" is significant here, as it suggests Wood plucked the example of James out of the air, when in fact James has been the laudatory model from the beginning. This fact becomes even more apparent in "The Digressionist," his largely negative review of Wallace's final story collection, *Oblivion*. Deeming the book "intolerable," Wood spends most of the review analyzing Wallace's prose, which for Wood does not blend cynicism and naiveté, or technical virtuosity and contemporary slang, as so many other reviewers have noted. Rather, Wallace's prose is "manically absorptive, endlessly soaking up the foul linguistic run-off of contemporary fluidity" (27, 26). This "immersive" strategy highlights the "moralist" streak in Wallace, as it highlights the "degree to which American consciousness has been colonized by advertising and all kinds of trivial media" (27). As a result, "his fictions strangely reproduce the extreme coldness that they abhor" (27). Once again, Wood contrasts Wallace's approach to that of James and finds the former wanting. James, in one of his prefaces, argues that although "relations stop nowhere," the artist's job is "to draw, by a geometry of his own, the circle within which they *appear* to do so" (28). For Wood, James's directive represents "one proper ideal of novelistic art," namely "the author's self-sacrificial stylistic collapse into the individual idiolects of his characters," which is a fancy way of describing the free indirect style (28). Wallace, by way of damning contrast, "too often ends up only collapsing into the collective idiolect of the culture that he is documenting" (28). As a result, "irony is starved to sarcasm, and sympathy to voyeurism" (29).[2]

To return to Wood's earlier categories, Wallace's immersive prose, coupled with his "moralist" outrage, places him in the Flaubertean tradition of correction or the comedy of fault-finding. As Wood puts

[2]For a pointed riposte of Wood's negative review, which includes one key instance of simple misreading, see Wyatt Mason's *Oblivion* review, "You Don't Like It? You Don't Have To Play," published in *London Review of Books*. My thanks to Stephen Burn for pointing me to Mason's piece.

it in *How Fiction Works*, Wallace's fiction "prosecutes an intense argument about the decomposition of language in America, and he is not afraid to decompose—and discompose—his own style in the interest of making us live through this linguistic America with him" (33). What Wood does not find in Wallace's work are human beings. In Wood's assessment, Wallace is interested in humans only "at the point at which they cede their humanity to the punitive conformity around them. [Wallace] backs into his characters, occupying the wake they leave behind as they disappear into American reality," a reality regarded always as a debased linguistic construct ("The Digressionist" 27).

This lengthy digression into Wood's complex critique of Wallace's work blueprints the various ways Messud appears to be sparring with Wallace and his influence on the post–baby boom generation. For while Bootie's experience with *Infinite Jest* and Amherst marks him as the character most directly associated with Wallace, other characters also intersect with various of Wallace's characteristic arguments and themes. Murray Thwaite, whom Bootie chooses as his spiritual "father" after abandoning *Infinite Jest*, also serves as a complex Oedipal figure for the novel's other titular "children." In other words, he is the father they all need somehow to "slay" in a dynamic that Messud overtly terms the "anxiety of influence" (177). What's more, the battle lines she draws between these children and their father dovetail with, and also interrogate, Wallace's articulation of his own antagonistic relationship with his postmodern forebears, specifically, and with the 1960s counterculture more broadly. And yet, contra Wallace (as perceived by Wood), the interrogation is never corrective but rather forgiving to both father and child.

In his early manifestos, including "Fictional Futures and the Conspicuously Young," "E Unibus Pluram," and the McCaffery interview, Wallace grounds his artistic project always in terms of a generational clash. The word "generation" appears twenty-six times in "Fictional Futures" and seventeen times in "E Unibus Pluram." In every case, Wallace is at pains to explain how *his* generation is uniquely different from that of his immediate predecessors. His generation is the "first for whom television was something to be lived with instead of just looked at" and the first generation "raised and nourished on messages equating what one consumes with who one is" (*Supposedly* 43). Conversely, the preceding generation of writers regarded television and pop culture as "at best an annoying tic and at worst a dangerous vapidity that compromises fiction's seriousness by dating it out of the Platonic Always where it ought to reside" (43). For Wallace, this divide is so great that "transgenerational discourse" breaks down (44). But Wallace also regarded his generation as paying the cultural and historical "price" for the baby boomer's anarchic excesses, as evidenced by his famous comparison of "the last few years of the postmodern era" with "the way you feel when you're in high school and your parents go on a trip and you throw a party . . . For awhile it's great, free and freeing, parental authority gone and overthrown . . . But then time passes . . . and you gradually start wishing your parents would come back and restore some fucking order in your house" (*Conversations* 52). He concludes this metaphor by explaining, "The postmodern founders' patricidal work was great, but patricide produces orphans" (52). Having admitted earlier in the same interview that John Barth, Robert Coover, Vladimir Nabokov, and Thomas Pynchon are the "patriarch[s] for [his] patricide" (48), Wallace here complains that his own patricidal work has left him longing for the authority of the father he's slayed. But this contradiction hardly invalidates Wallace's argument, for the contradiction is already baked into the Oedipal model from which he drew his terms. We long for the approval of the father we slay.

Messud's portrait of her characters and their conflicted relationship to Murray deftly captures the contradictions, intended or not, imbedded in Wallace's "patricidal" model of the artistic generation gap. Bootie's relationship with Murray perfectly follows this pattern. Before his experience in New York, Bootie regards Murray as "in every admirable way, extraordinary," and his journey to New York is nothing less than an audition for discipleship: "His uncle was, without question, a great man; and Bootie would try to be worthy of him" (59, 62). Whereas in Wallace's artistic trajectory his "postmodern forebears" are responsible for ushering in the ironic era, in cultural terms his immediate predecessors are the baby boomers who protested the Vietnam War only to grow out of their idealism and vote for Ronald Reagan, a transformation he chronicles in great detail in his posthumous novel *The Pale King*. Murray Thwaite embodies the baby boomer ethos against which Wallace defined himself, an antagonism that also drives the patricidal plot of Messud's novel. A child of the 1960s, Murray cut his journalistic teeth covering John F. Kennedy's trip to Berlin and the Civil Rights movement in the American South (54). Now he is a wealthy, self-satisfied womanizer with a spacious apartment overlooking Central Park. Nevertheless, without a hint of irony or self-consciousness, he continues to consider himself a bastion of "integrity," a word he applies to himself, or has it applied to him, nearly half a dozen times over the course of the novel. "Integrity," Murray tells a star-struck interviewer, "is everything, it's all you've got" (55). Similarly, Bootie, pondering how he might "present himself" to Murray "as a kind of disciple," describes his uncle as "a man who had chosen the path of the mind, who had opted for integrity over glory, even if," Bootie tellingly notes, this path "had brought him fame" (107). Murray also considers himself a noble "truth-teller" and a tireless advocate for "truthfulness" more broadly (371, 330). By trading Wallace for Murray and *Infinite Jest* for *War and Peace*, Bootie effectively works backward through Wallace's linear model of generational conflict. Bootie's confrontation with Murray also represents his confrontation with the baby boomer legacy.

Bootie becomes disillusioned with Murray when, after becoming his uncle's "amanuensis" (195), he discovers the banal platitudes that constitute *How to Live*. In another nod to Wallace, Bootie describes his disappointment as a form of "unease, dis-ease," that hyphenated last word being a direct reference to a passage from *Infinite Jest* wherein an AA sponsor writes down the word "DISEASE on a sheet of paper and then divide[s] and hyphenate[s] the word so that it becomes *DIS-EASE*" (*Emperor* 239, *IJ* 203). Bootie decides to deal with his disillusionment by writing a vicious exposé of his hero. He becomes, in the novel's terminology, "a young Turk needing to slay his father" (177). But the person he most hopes to please in this endeavor is no less than Murray himself. As he sees it, his exposure of Murray's hollowness functions as an act of "truth-telling" and ethical "integrity" that will earn him Murray's approval. He even binds the exposé into a black plastic cover and presents it to his hero (332). When Murray explodes and, effectively, disowns him as son and disciple, Bootie meekly insists, "I was only doing what you wanted me to. Following instructions, almost" (338–39).

Messud's irony works on numerous levels here. If Wallace's own predilection for home-spun life advice is in fact a target of the *How to Live* motif, then Bootie's disappointment could be read as the first clear critique of Wallace's project. Although Bootie regards the clichéd simplicities of *How to Live* as unworthy of Murray's groundbreaking political interventions, Messud's portrait suggests that they are what lie behind the earnestness that drove Murray's 1960s work in the first place. These same simplicities mirror what might very well emerge from the "anti-rebels" who, in Wallace's vision, eschew metawatching and affirm single-entendre values. In this regard, Messud might have in mind Wallace's repeated affirmation of the value of banal common sense. Don Gately, a recovering heroin addict at a halfway house called Ennett House and one of the unquestioned heroes of *Infinite Jest*, observes that the "clichéd directives" that constitute the heart of AA "are a lot more deep and hard to actually *do*" (273). Gately also argues that, "even if they are just clichés, clichés are (a) soothing, and (b) remind you of common sense, and (c) license the universal assent that drowns out silence; and (4) silence is deadly . . . if you've got the Disease" (278). David Letzler is almost alone among Wallace's professional critics in asking why so many of Wallace's readers have accepted Gately's ameliorative championing of banality:

> Why on earth is this philosophy of simplistic language and conformity so celebrated by English professors—by *readers of David Foster Wallace*, no less? If the Wallace critics who vaunt the Ennet mindset were presented in any other setting with these notions about the evils of polysyllables and the pure good of the *Reader's Digest*, they would roll their eyes or laugh, and rightly so. (Letzler 143)

Although Letzler answers his own question by suggesting that the "empty, easy clichés provide relief from the near-unreadable manic overload in the novel's other sections," his original charge remains largely unanswered (143). Via Bootie's disillusionment with his hero, Messud might be making a charge similar to Letzler's. In the same way that one might register disapproval that a novel as "original and thought-dense" as *Infinite Jest* rests on a bedrock of clichés, so, too, might Bootie feel betrayed that a mind as ostensibly capacious as Murray's could ultimately be a repository of banalities. However, in Messud's layered "comedy of forgiveness," Bootie's insight does not result in a "corrective" critique of either Murray or Wallace, for Bootie's admiration for Murray, and his desire for Murray's approval, remain.

But Bootie isn't the only character with conflicted father issues as regards Murray. If the novel has a villain, it is the Australian magazine publisher Ludovic Seeley, who is repeatedly called a "snake" (273, 299, 376). In the novel's carefully orchestrated Edenic motif, Ludo, like the serpent in the Garden, "believes in debunking" the authority of the father (342). Drawing upon the novel's title, he hopes to "show people the Murray Thwaite is the Wizard of Oz, a tiny, pointless man roaring behind a curtain"; in short, "the emperor has no clothes" (123). In his view, Murray is a "sentimentalist" who "hasn't got an original idea in his head" (122, 121). Ultimately, Ludo is an agent of cynicism and irony, a proponent of the view, to quote Rosenblatt again, that "nothing was to be believed in or taken seriously. Nothing was real." Ludo is first described as possessing a "Nabokovian brow," and is later deemed "ironic and suave" (4, 215). He hopes that his magazine, the *Monitor*, will launch a "cynic's revolution" designed to strip away the sanctimonious pretentiousness of the New York literary set, as typified by Murray. His fiancé Marina Thwaite wonders if, "when it came to Seeley, 'genuine' was a word with any currency at all" (177).

But as with Wallace and his own conflicted relationship with his 1960s postmodern forebears, Ludo's disdain for Murray is built upon a dialectical dependency. Ludo freely admits that Murray is "an important figure in [his] formation" (178). Marina can't help but notice that though "he appeared so powerfully to disdain the older man," he still "clamored to meet him" (177). More than that, Ludo marries the man's daughter, a clear attempt to displace Murray from his Oedipal role. Danielle, the fourth of the novel's "children," notes with distaste that "Marina seemed like [Murray's] lover" (254). Similarly, when Ludo admonishes Marina to crawl out of her father's shadow, he prophesies that she will feel "a relief almost sexual" (225). Although Murray cannot stand Ludo, treating him exactly like a romantic rival, Marina notes that he often "sounded to her . . . oddly like her father," a view supported by Marina's mother, who says of Ludo, just prior to the wedding, "He reminds me, in some ways, of your father" (226, 252).

The 9/11 terrorist attacks scuttle Ludo's hoped-for "cynic's revolution." By noon of that unforgettable Tuesday, Ludo realizes, "We are completely fucked" (416). Perhaps obliquely referencing those numerous post-9/11 predictions of the Death of Irony, Messud depicts Ludo forlornly examining the cover of his inaugural issue, which features a "remarkable photograph of a sunburst, the idea having been that they were exploding upon the scene, illuminating truths," and conceding that "already it looked out of date and faintly forlorn, like some child's abandoned artwork" (417).

But the novel does not simply shoo Ludo aside, in some sort of implicit solidarity with Rosenblatt and Carter, for Murray, the figure of earnestness and truth and integrity, has already been exposed as an emperor with no clothes. Bootie regards 9/11 as "an end to false idols" and, seeing Murray as "emperor in this place of pretense," predicts that his hero "would be toppled" by 9/11 (437). But in one of the novel's most provocative ironic turns, Murray's reputation is burnished by the attacks. After watching the second tower fall, Bootie disappears to Miami, in effect staging his own death. In his writings following the attacks, Murray refuses to turn "hawk," despite the fact that news reports repeatedly note that the fallen towers "killed" his nephew. At Bootie's funeral, Murray, who feels directly responsible for the death, "couldn't help but be aware of the irony that Bootie's death had granted him greater nobility, an importance—he knew it to be false—as a man of justice, unswayed by the arrows of misfortune" (461).

So while Messud dramatizes how the 9/11 attacks might have punctured a hole in the placenta of smug irony that permeated the popular culture in the years immediately preceding, her novel also questions the prevailing narrative that the attacks granted the United States a new "moral clarity," to quote William Bennet's hagiography of George W. Bush. The novel refutes the simple either/or that pits irony against earnestness, cynicism against sentimentality, but does so without the tortured contortions of Wallace's highly self-conscious sincerity. If her cynics at root are sentimentalists, then so, too, are her sentimentalists cynics, "liars" and "actors" (406). Rather than debunk her characters for their contradictions, Messud uses the layered irony of her Jamesean narrative style to give her character fleeting moments of "clarity," a word that appears in its various forms (clarity, clear-eyed, etc.) at nearly a dozen key moments in the novel. Significantly, Bootie ends the novel by registering at the Clarion hotel. Each character, at one point or another, experiences a moment of "clarity" that, in a more sentimental novel, would have resulted in correction.

But here, these moments often make no real difference. Clarity does not result in improvement. To paraphrase Wood's assessment of Austen's art, which *The Emperor's Children* vividly invokes, Messud's characters "are not mocked but gradually comprehended and finally forgiven" (14). In this way, Messud also gently refutes Wallace's blanket claim that irony only "has emergency use" and is "singularly unuseful when it comes to constructing anything to replace the hypocrisies it debunks" (*Supposedly* 67). Messud's novel suggests that irony, when employed in the Jamesean narrative mode, provides a way to expose both cynicism and sentimentality while also preserving the flawed but forgiven "human beings" whose faults have been so deftly but also gently disclosed. Keeble is right in noting that "things do not fundamentally change despite major disruptions in the characters' personal lives, nor does the ostensible new seriousness of life after 9/11 shed light on these disruptions" (371). Both Keeble and David Simpson cannot decide if this failure to change should be read as "a tribute to the resilience of ordinary life or a more damning indictment of the sheer indifference and self-centeredness of the homeland mainstream" (216). In light of the novel's sustained and deliberate ambiguity, and its blending of critique and empathy, perhaps the correct answer is that Messud is making both points, simultaneously, with the difference that Messud isn't really addressing the "homeland mainstream" but rather the unique particulars of her characters.

As Keeble notes, the one exception to this pattern is Bootie, who stages his own death and reinvents himself in Florida, with a brand new name and, presumably, a new identity. Keeble argues that the change is merely cosmetic, because Bootie still retains the same desire he had before 9/11, namely to make his mark as a writer of note, and yet I would add that his final change is merely one of three key transformations that shape Bootie, each one marked by the book he is reading at the time. Of the four key texts that shape him, the one that remains constant is a collection of Emerson essays, suggesting that Bootie retains a core self upon which he remains reliant. But the other three texts he takes up not only help us understand his changing identity but also provide perhaps the last component of Messud's fascinating dialogue with Wallace.

As noted above, Bootie trades *Infinite Jest* for *War and Peace*, which occupies him for the bulk of his time in New York, when he works as Murray's amanuensis. The shift from Wallace's epic novel of postmodern self-obsession to Tolstoy's even more epic social portrait signals Messud's championing of redemptive comedy over Wallace's hermetic moralism. Wood himself argues that Messud's mode is "the wonderful creation of the late nineteenth- and early twentieth-century novel" (*Irresponsible* 10). Bootie's progress through the New York social world also parallels Tolstoy's novel in comic ways, with Bootie identifying himself with brooding "Pierre wandering Moscow" (242) with his love interest, the vivacious Marina, standing in as the novel's Natasha. What's more, Ludo's magazine, the *Monitor*, takes its name from Napoleon's paper (192), suggesting that 9/11 is the Russian winter that finally stopped the French emperor.

After Murray disowns him, Bootie steals a copy of Robert Musil's *The Man without Qualities*, the final encyclopedic novel Messud overtly places alongside *Infinite Jest*. Bootie even assumes the name of Musil's titular character, Ulrich, when he reinvents himself in South Florida. Whereas the allegedly "dead" Bootie gets elevated by the same people who scorned him as a "better person," someone possessed of "'Gravitas,' 'ambition,' 'integrity,'" each word framed in scare quotes (453), the newly invented Ulrich, from his perch in the Clarion hotel in South Beach, is a clean slate, a man without qualities but full of possibility. If *War and Peace* serves as a sharp contrast to Wallace's insular epic, then Musil's unfinished novel might be viewed more as a partner work. Like Wallace, Musil built his reputation as both a novelist and a supremely gifted essayist. Similarly, his unfinished masterpiece has long been associated with the work of the philosophical essayists of the early twentieth century, who, as David Luft explains, moved the novel "away from the story and immediate aesthetic totality in the direction of essayism, interpretation, and fragmented form" (18). Luft's description also applies to Wallace's great novel. By having Bootie begin with Wallace, move through Tolstoy, and end with the deeply intellectual modernist Musil, Messud deftly registers her critique of Wallace's work while also providing an august pedigree for Wallace's achievement. Like Bootie, Wallace, in Messud's narrative, is a writer of ambition and gravitas but also one who possibly still hasn't reached his full potential.

5

Competitive Friendship

Love and Reckoning in Jonathan Franzen's *Freedom*

Of all the writers most directly associated with David Foster Wallace's fictional project, none can claim a more intimate association than Jonathan Franzen. As early as 1996, Wallace openly described himself and Franzen as "friends, and sort of rivals" who argued affably but intensely about the purposes and potential future direction of fiction ("*Quo Vadis*—Introduction" 8). Franzen has long supported that view, a position borne out by the voluminous correspondence between himself and Wallace that D. T. Max cites in his Wallace biography, as well as by Franzen's numerous public eulogies to his deceased friend, the most prominent of which, "Farther Away," served as the title piece of his 2012 essay collection. But the connection goes beyond mere friendship. In *Jonathan Franzen at the End of Postmodernism*, Stephen J. Burn argues extensively that Franzen's fiction should be read directly alongside that of Wallace and Richard Powers, the two most prominent figures associated with the ongoing attempt to move US literary fiction beyond postmodernism (Burn 16). Franzen's relationship to Wallace was therefore threefold. As he observes in "Farther Away," "David and I had a friendship of compare and contrast and (in a brotherly way) compete" (*Farther* 40).

Wallace's 2008 suicide hit Franzen particularly hard. On one level, he lost a dear friend. On another, he lost serious ground in his ongoing (brotherly) competition with Wallace. "Farther Away" is quite frank in its depiction of what Franzen calls his "fleeing grief and enduring anger at David's death," but even more striking is Franzen's bitter accusation that one of the precipitating factors leading to Wallace's suicide was Wallace's "loathsome hunger for career advantage" (42). In his 2010 bestseller, *Freedom*, much of which was composed in the wake of Wallace's suicide, Franzen works through, in fictional form, his complex feelings about Wallace and their competitive friendship. When read alongside "Farther Away," which operates as something of a Rosetta stone for the novel's coded engagement with Wallace, *Freedom* represents, as Franzen puts it, "a mapping of the writers' experience onto a waking dream" and a "less than strictly historical kind of truth"— namely, "the novelist's 'truth'" (*Farther* 32).

Freedom is the story of an intense male friendship between Walter Berglund, a solemn, progressive environmentalist, and his rock-star college roommate, the cynical womanizer Richard Katz. The friendship is complicated by a third figure, Walter's wife Patty, an intense, depressive college athlete and stay-at-home mom on whom both men are erotically fixated. Published a year before Eugenides' *The Marriage Plot*, Franzen's novel anticipates that work in casting its allegory of artistic anxiety as a love triangle, in which the dogged and earnest Walter must square off against his more charismatic, sexually appealing rival. Katz, like Eugenides' Leonard Bankhead, bears several character traits connecting him to Wallace, while Walter occupies the Franzen role in much the same way Mitchell Grammaticus invokes Eugenides. Remarkably, Franzen's novel stages its drama in dialogue with two of the primary texts that also inform Claire Messud's exploration of Wallace's work—namely, Leo Tolstoy's *War and Peace*, which Patty reads at the cusp of her betrayal of Walter with Katz, and Robert Musil's *The Man without Qualities*, which also dramatizes an extended romantic rivalry between three longtime companions: Ulrich, the mercurial title character, and his married friends Clarissa and Walter, the latter of whom might have provided Franzen with the name of his own main character. While the three novels interlock in a fascinating kaleidoscope of shared intertextual engagements, *Freedom* is the most charged and emotionally affecting of the trio, an intensity grounded in its author's intimate connection to Wallace as well as in Franzen's bareboned determination, as he observed about Wallace's own fiction, to give his readers "the worst of himself" (*Farther* 39). "If you really love fiction," Franzen has insisted elsewhere, "you'll find the only pages worth keeping are the ones that reflect you as you really are" (*Farther* 10).

In "Farther Away," Franzen obliquely refers to writing *Freedom* in a "state of flight" from himself that began "soon after David's death" (19). As he puts it, "I'd made a conscious decision not to deal with the hideous suicide of someone I'd loved so much but instead to take refuge in anger and work" (19–20). Only after weaving his "waking dream" and disclosing his "less than strictly historical kind of truth" was he ready to confront Wallace's suicide directly. Franzen describes a solitary trip he took to the island of Masafuera off the coast of Chile, the site of Daniel Defoe's *Robinson Crusoe*. Once stranded there, alone, amid the desolate fog, he reads Defoe's novel, scatters a portion of Wallace's ashes, and works through his grief. But Franzen also uses the essay as an occasion to analyze the rise of the realistic novel in Europe and the United States and its connection to the burgeoning emergence of bourgeois individuality. Ultimately, Franzen links Wallace's suicide to his friend's isolation and solipsistic self-hatred, both of which Wallace's work sought valiantly to combat.

Although the essay provides an intimate, deeply personal, and nuanced portrait of Wallace, the author of *The Corrections* also seeks in this piece to provide a "corrective" to some of the more simplistically laudatory visions of Wallace that emerged in the wake of Wallace's death. "The people who knew David least well," he observes midway through, "are most likely to speak of him in saintly terms" (*Farther* 39). That saintly image, Franzen argues, fails to account for the clear indications of his own failings that Wallace disclosed in his work. For instance, Franzen observes that "close loving relationships . . . have no standing in the Wallace fictional universe"; instead, his fiction is replete with "characters scheming to *appear* loving or to prove to themselves that what feels like love is really just disguised self-interest" (39). Wallace also reveals "the extremes of his own narcissism, misogyny, compulsiveness, self-deception, dehumanizing moralism and theologizing, doubt in the possibility of love, and entrapment in footnotes-within-footnotes self-consciousness" (39). This catalog comports with

Franzen's personal analysis of Wallace's suicide as resulting from Wallace's sense that "he never quite felt that he deserved to receive" love: Wallace, in short, "was a lifelong prisoner on the island of himself" (41). According to this reading, Wallace's calculated suicide represented "a capitulation to the side of himself that his embattled better side perceived as evil" and further confirmed "the justice of the death sentence" (42).

Ultimately, though, Franzen's analysis, however accurate or inaccurate it might be, cannot be decoupled from his ongoing artistic competition with Wallace, a point Franzen makes little effort to conceal. Despite Wallace's revelation that he and Franzen "argued" about the purpose of fiction, one point Franzen insists they agreed upon was their shared belief "that fiction is a solution, the *best* solution, to the problem of existential solitude"; it is a "way off the island" (44). Here Franzen is clearly invoking one of Wallace's most famous directives for the purpose of fiction, as spelled out in Wallace's 1993 McCaffery interview:

> I guess a big part of serious fiction's purpose is to give the reader, who like all of us is sort of marooned in her own skull, to give her imaginative access to other selves . . . If a piece of fiction can allow us imaginatively to identify with a character's pain, we might then also more easily conceive of others identifying with our own. This is nourishing, redemptive; we become less alone inside. (21–22)

It is difficult to imagine that Franzen did not have this very same, and widely quoted, passage in mind, with its memorable metaphor of the reader "marooned in her own skull," when he chose to analyze Wallace's tragic solipsism in the context of a solo trip to Robinson Crusoe's famous island. Franzen extends the metaphor when he speaks to the value of Wallace's art, which he describes as a life raft for the reader. "To the extent that each of us is stranded on his or her own existential island," Franzen posits, "we gratefully seized on each new dispatch from that farthest-away island which was David" (39). But at the end of his life, Wallace had grown "bored with his own tricks" and was "unable to muster enough excitement about his new novel to find a way forward with it" (44). In light of his and Wallace's ongoing literary "competition," Wallace had failed as a writer, and yet, at the precise moment of Franzen's triumph by default, Wallace turned himself into not only "a very public legend" but also a "benignant and morally clairvoyant artist/saint" (38). Franzen's final valedictory to his friend attempts to accept both his personal and his professional loss: "David had chosen to leave the people who loved him and give himself to the world of the novel and its readers, and I was ready to wish him well in it" (48).

During the early publicity push for *Freedom*, Franzen attributed his inspiration to his growing acceptance of himself as an adult, a process that began with the death of his parents and which was exacerbated, as he murmured to Terry Gross, by Wallace's suicide. "It's probably the biggest thing that changed," he observed, referring to his new embrace of his maturity. "There was—the death of my friend David Wallace might have been a part of that, as well . . . It wasn't enough to lose my parents" ("Jonathan Franzen on the Book").[1] He goes on to explain, "Coinciding with turning 50 and feeling how fortunate I was to still be alive and how fortunate I was to still have the capacity to write, I think that had a lot to do with that sudden turn toward feeling my own age" ("Jonathan Franzen on the Book"). Although the trailing ellipses might be a product of his lasting grief, they might also suggest his wariness about making too overt a link between the novel's composition and his feelings about Wallace. For it is certainly possible to make too much of Wallace's presence in the book. Nevertheless, Franzen has left so indelible a trail of clues, both via "Farther Away" and through the correspondence he supplied to D. T. Max, that it is also difficult to ignore that presence, or to resist sifting through those clues. As with Eugenides' somewhat disingenuous denials regarding his character

---

[1] Five years after the book's publication, Franzen proved to be much less reticent than he was earlier about inviting the reading offered in this essay when he described the novel's early conception in an essay published in the *Gaurdian*. He describes how the first real breakthrough in his writing corresponded directly with the news of Wallace's first unsuccessful suicide attempt. He goes on to say,

> The exact coincidence of his attempt and my breakthrough seemed uncanny. It still seems uncanny. Dave and I had been very close for many years, and sometimes I feel as if he and I were a single unit that split in two in 2008: as if the force of his downward movement, into severe depression and death, were matched on my side by an upward surge of liberation and renewed life. The day after his second memorial service, in Manhattan, I started writing *Freedom* in earnest. A year later, it was finished. ("Modern Life")

Leonard Bankhead's connection to Wallace, Franzen's careful evasiveness represents simply the artist's prerogative not to do the interpretive work that is the reader's responsibility.

Richard Katz's various invocations of David Foster Wallace are dispersed throughout the novel and involve both direct clues and references as well as more diffuse aspects of character and plot. Like Eugenides' Leonard Bankhead, Franzen's Katz shares Wallace's now famous addiction to Skoal dipping tobacco (99–101, 348). Early on, Patty describes him as "self-absorbed" and "addiction-prone" (66). Franzen bestows on Richard Wallace's pockmarked skin, which in Wallace's case resulted from an adolescent bout of bad acne that, according to D. T. Max, Wallace battled obsessively with Clearasil well into his college years (20). The walls of Richard's bedroom are painted black, a clear allusion to Wallace's own black-walled writing room in his Bloomington home (*Freedom* 103, Max 232). Richard also shares Wallace's bulk. Eliza, Patty's neurotic, heroine-addicted college friend, describes him as "so big, it's like being rolled over by a neutron star. It's like being erased with a giant eraser" (66). Patty picks up on that last metaphor and, in the weeks leading up to her finally meeting him, refers to him as "the giant eraser" (66). When Patty finally meets "the eraser," he is reading Thomas Pynchon's *V.* (67).

But the most prominent component of Richard's character is his sexual promiscuity, and his unstoppable sexual allure to women, Patty in particular. Whereas Eugenides portrays the sexually alluring Leonard Bankhead as a gallant prince and intense listener, Katz is a cynical, unrepentant womanizer who refers to women throughout the novel as "chicks." Max amply chronicles Wallace's own promiscuity, which "had been a part of his life for a long time" but which shifted into overdrive after he became famous following the publication of *Infinite Jest* (232). Franzen obliquely references the darker side of Wallace's promiscuity in "Farther Away" when he disingenuously elects to "pass over the question . . . of how such a beautiful human being had come by such vividly intimate knowledge of the thoughts of hideous men," that last phrase a clear reference to Wallace's story series "Brief Interviews with Hideous Men," which is an exhaustive catalog of the varieties of male misogyny (43). Franzen suggests that those who, like perhaps Eugenides in his portrait of Leonard, "took [Wallace's] laborious hyperconsideratenss and moral wisdom at face value" did so because they had "only glancing formal contact with him" (39). Franzen leaves no doubt about the real-life source of Richard's damaging promiscuity when he has Richard observe to Walter, "Sometimes I think my purpose on earth is to put my penis in the vaginas of as many women as I can," a line Franzen extracted word-for-word from a letter he received from Wallace and which he allowed Max to quote directly (*Freedom* 142, Max 232). In one final nod to Wallace, Franzen links Richard's promiscuity to drug addiction. In penance for sleeping with Patty, for instance, Katz tries celibacy and observes that "abjuring sex had seemed like the natural complement to staying clean of drugs and alcohol" (197).

In a similar vein, Franzen equips Walter with a variety of characteristics that point back to himself.[2] Although in his *Fresh Air* interview Franzen revealed that one of the models for Walter and Patty's marriage was that of his parents, he also explains, "I wanted to set [the novel] in times contemporaneous with my own. So in that way, too, I turned my parents into people my age; into people I might be or I might know . . . It was something that came from inside" ("Jonathan Franzen on the Book"). While the inner details of his parents' marriage are known only to Franzen, he has been fairly open about the collapse of his own first marriage, both in the concluding essay of his memoir, *The Discomfort Zone* titled "My Bird Problem" and in his 2011 Commencement Address at Kenyon College, the exact site of Wallace's now famous 2005 Commencement Address, since published as *This Is Water*. Like Franzen and his ex-wife, Walter and Patty marry early, directly out of college: according to his own account, Franzen got married in the fall of 1982, when he was twenty-three, while Patty and Walter get married "three weeks after [Patty's] college graduation," in the summer of 1982 (*Farther* 131, *Freedom* 119).

---

[2]Mark Bresnan, in an essay exploring the role of punk and independent music in the novel, provides a fascinating counter-reading in which Katz, not Walter, serves as "an avatar of his author" (32). He connects Katz's cynical discomfort with his unexpected popularity following the release of his *Nameless Lake* album to Franzen's dust up with Oprah Winfrey during *The Corrections'* brief turn as an Oprah Book Club selection. Bresnan speculates that Katz's long slog in the periphery of the rock-music mainstream can be read as an expression of Franzen's own belated desire to operate within a "different model for publishing and marketing—a literary analogue for the independent record labels for which Richard works, the type of publishing house that would never think of encouraging its writers to appear on *The Oprah Winfrey Show*" (35).

In addition, Walter shares Franzen's environmentalist obsessions, which also follow Franzen's personal trajectory. As he explains in his Kenyon address, Franzen's fury at the damage being done to the environment made him increasingly "angrier and people-hating"; after his marriage began to crumble, he made a conscious decision to "stop worrying about the environment," a decision that held sway until, as he puts it, "A funny thing happened . . . I fell in love with birds" (*Farther* 12). Walter's demise begins when he foolishly signs on with a rich, bird-loving proponent of Mountain Top Removal, thinking he can develop an environmentally sound process of "managed reclamation" that "could mitigate far more of the damage than people realized" (*Freedom* 211). After Walter is betrayed by the developer and destroys his career as well as his marriage, he devotes himself to saving birds from his neighbors' murderous cats. Walter's relentless anger about the environment also recalls that of Franzen's early protagonist, *Strong Motion*'s Louis Holland. These autobiographical echoes do not reduce Walter to an authorial double, for Walter, unlike the childless Franzen, has children early and is depicted as a devoted, though certainly imperfect, father. Rather, Franzen bestows these details on Walter the way Nabokov "bestowed on the characters of [his] novels some treasured items of [his] past" (95). And although Franzen has insisted that he has published no "more than twenty or thirty pages of scenes drawn directly from real-life events," he nevertheless affirms, "My fiction is extremely autobiographical," going on to explain that his "conception of a novel is that it ought to be a personal struggle, a direct and total engagement with the author's story of his or her own life" (*Farther* 128–29).

The complex, competitive friendship, and overtly brotherly bond, between Richard and Walter—Patty argues the bond between them was a "sibling thing"— functions as *Freedom*'s central conflict (131). So far, the majority of the novel's professional readers have regarded that conflict as a synecdoche for the novel's larger social, ethical, and political concerns. Catherine Walker Bergström reads the novel through the lens of Emmanuel Levinas's ethics of recognition. For Bergström, the Patty/Walter/Richard love triangle is a central expression of the novel's affirmation of a vision of freedom that must be squared with what Levinas calls "the love of obligations," which love Patty comes "to recognize as paradoxically liberating" (117). Áine Mahon invites us to read that conflict as a means by which readers enter into a stage of "imaginative intimacy" with Franzen's flawed characters, all in accordance with Richard Rorty's programmatic call for an ethically grounded form of literary reading designed to "decrease our self-centeredness by reminding us that others are in pain—pain of a sort which we may be likely to cause, or which we might be able to relieve" (qtd. in Mahon 91). These readings and other like them remind us that the novel is about a great many things—freedom, for one. Nevertheless, Franzen also clearly uses the Richard/Walter relationship as a fictionalized proxy for his own complex feelings about his and Wallace's friendship, and their professional rivalry. Franzen's frank account of that friendship, and his analysis of Wallace's suicide and its possible "career advancement" motive, guard such a reading from the charge of intentional fallacy. More importantly, Franzen provides a wide range of textual evidence within the novel to support such an interpretation.

The first telling clue is Patty's early reference to Richard as "the eraser." She repeats the phrase when she enters his black bedroom, which, as we've already seen, Franzen based on Wallace's black-walled writing room in Bloomington. Whereas the rest of their shared suite is immaculately ordered, on Walter's insistence, Richard's black bedroom displays a brand of "punk disorder that Walter's influence had suppressed in the living room" (103). In addition to the "overloaded bookshelves," she notes "several cans of spit" and "dangled dark bedsheets that it was interesting and somehow not unpleasant to think that Eliza had been vigorously erased in" (103). The implication is clear: Richard's black bedroom, site of his sexual conquests, stands in for Wallace's black writing room, from whence issued the oversized, culture-devouring work that in various ways sought to "erase" all literary competitors, Franzen included. Metaphors matter. To cite Wallace's personal bête noire, John Barth,

A fine metaphor, simile, or other figure of speech, in addition to its obvious "first-order" relevance to the thing it describes, will be seen upon reflection to have a second order significance: it may be drawn from the *milieu* of the action, for example, or be particularly appropriate to the sensibility of the narrator, even hinting to the reader things of which the narrator is unaware. (*Lost in the Funhouse* 74)

The metaphor of Richard as "the eraser" begins with Eliza and gets picked up by Patty in her third-person autobiography. Neither character necessarily knows at what the second-order significance might be hinting. All that matters is that the reader gets the hint.[3]

Intriguingly, both Eugenides and Franzen figure Wallace's literary power as sexual potency. From the beginning of his career, Wallace freely drew upon, and was also critical of, the longtime conflation of the male writer's "pen" with his "penis." In *Broom of the System*, Wallace bestows upon Lenore Stonecipher's neurotic, sexually impotent lover the comic name Rick Vigorous. What's more, Vigorous spends much of the novel trying to compensate for his sexual inadequacy by telling Lenore long comic stories that he falsely claims are paraphrases of story submissions he receives at the *Frequent Review*, a literary magazine of which he is the editor. As mentioned in Chapter 3, Wallace was also consistent—"to the point of affection," according to Clare Hayes-Brady—in referring to his imagined readers as female (133). In a significant unforced error, Wallace, during his televised interview with Charlie Rose following the publication of *A Supposedly Fun Thing I'll Never Do Again*, defended *Infinite Jest*'s immense size by suggesting that he, too, has a problem with "size." But just as Rose begins to ask his next question, a clearly agitated Wallace adds, "Feminists are all saying this—so feminists are saying that all white males go, 'Okay, I'm going to sit down and write this enormous book and impose my phallus on the consciousness of the world' . . . And if that was going on, it was going on at a level of awareness that I do not want access to" ("Interview"). He revisits this complaint in his infamous takedown of John Updike when he claims he has heard readers refer to Updike as "just a penis with a thesaurus," after which he freely refers to Updike and his contemporaries Mailer and Roth as "famous phallocrats" (*Consider* 52–53).

Conversely, Franzen is quite conscious of what he is doing when he reveals, in "Farther Away," that, a few years before his death, Wallace sent signed copies of his two most recent books to Franzen, with telling additions: "On the title page of one of them, [Wallace]

---

[3]Bergström reads the metaphor in terms of Levinas's analysis of carnal desire as articulated in *Totality and Infinity*, where he argues, "In the carnel [relation . . .], the body quits the status of an existent" (qtd. in Bergström 120).

traced the outline of his hand; on the title page of the other was an outline of an erection so huge that it ran off the page, annotated with a little arrow and the remark 'scale 100%'" (40). The drawings were clearly meant in jest, but only just, for Franzen provides this detail immediately after admitting that his and Wallace's friendship was one of "compare and contrast and (in a brotherly way) compete" (40). Franzen knew what Wallace meant. So although Wallace was at pains to separate himself from the "phallocrats" of the previous generation—and surely this was the purpose of his public slaying of John Updike—he was nevertheless not always immune from equating his own literary power in sexual terms.

Richard Katz's first name, therefore, is as pointed and suggestive as his last. There is nothing subtle about Franzen's repeated invitations to apply the diminutive "dick" to his Richard—a connection Wallace himself humorously invoked with his own Rick Vigorous. Richard assigns his sexual power to his "prophetic dick, his divining rod," which points him in Patty's direction and drives him to a betrayal he appears unable to resist. After he chooses to give Walter the copy of Patty's autobiography, which details their adulterous tryst, he thinks to himself, "So, my friend, . . . that's the end of you and me. You won that one, old buddy" (379). He then justifies his gesture by conceding, "His job in life was to speak the dirty truth. To be the dick" (378). But as the ramifications of what he has done begin to settle in, he feels drawn to suicide, namely by jumping from the Francis Scott Key Bridge in Georgetown, "the center of American world domination" (378). And as he ponders this option he thinks, "Had death, in fact, been his dick's message in sending him to Washington? Had he simply misunderstood its prophecy?" (379). Franzen sums up this motif—to the point of affectation—by following Richard back to his Jersey City apartment, where Richard calls up one of his abandoned bandmates, only to be called a "Dickhead" three times in succession (379).

His sexual betrayal of Walter is also intertwined with literary and artistic references that connect that betrayal to Wallace's and Franzen's literary rivalry. Although neither Richard nor Walter is a writer, they are both voracious readers. In particular, Richard is a fan of the Austrian novelist Thomas Bernhard, "his favorite new writer" (204). Bernhard's oeuvre boasts a number of clues connecting Richard's fandom back to the Franzen/Wallace rivalry. Bernhard's fourth novel, *Correction*, recalls Franzen's breakthrough book, *The Corrections*, while the Austrian's eighth novel, *Wittgenstein's Nephew*, invites comparisons not only to Wallace's Wittgenstein-inflected *Broom of the System* but also to David Markson's *Wittgenstein's Mistress*, for which Wallace published a rapturous, and oft-cited, review in 1990 titled "The Empty Plenum: David Markson's *Wittgenstein's Mistress*," later reprinted in Wallace's posthumous essay collection, *Both Flesh and Not* (73– 116). Bernhard was also drawn to the dramatic monologue, a mode that Wallace repeatedly employed in such later works as the "Brief Interviews" suite, "The Soul is Not a Smithy," "Good Old Neon," "Another Pioneer," and the much-lauded "Chris Fogel" novella included in *The Pale King*.

Bernhard's presence in *Freedom* might also be sourced to another episode of literary rivalry, this time between Franzen and fellow novelist Ben Marcus. In "Why Experimental Fiction Threatens to Destroy Publishing, Jonathan Franzen, and Life As We Know It: A Correction," Marcus mentions Bernhard's *Correction* in the context of his over-the-top rebuttal of Franzen's 2002 *New Yorker* essay "Mr. Difficult." In the latter piece, while ostensibly analyzing his own failure to warm to the fiction of William Gaddis, one of Wallace's most prominent artistic forebears, Franzen divides literary fiction into two competing models. The first is the Status model, "which was championed by Flaubert," and which holds that "the best novels are great works of art, the people who manage to write them deserve extraordinary credit, and if the average reader rejects the work it's because the average reader is a philistine" (100). The second is the Contract model wherein "a novel represents a compact between the writer and the reader, with the writer providing words out of which the reader creates a pleasurable experience" (100). He goes on to explain that, for Status adherents, "difficulty signals excellence; it suggests the novel's author has distained cheap compromise and stayed true to an artistic vision" (100). Conversely, for Contract writers, among whose number Franzen firmly counts himself, "difficulty is a sign of trouble" whereby the author is guilty of "placing his selfish artistic imperatives or his personal vanity ahead of the audience's legitimate desire to be entertained—of being, in other words, an asshole" (100). In his response to Franzen's piece, Marcus, a Status author, takes personal umbrage at Franzen's portrait of his Status compatriots, accusing Franzen of working up "a tight stranglehold on writers outside of the mainstream";

Marcus then speculates that Franzen is so angry at Status authors either "because he truly loathes their work or covets the kind of art-historical accolade they can draw" (43). Taking an implicit shot at Franzen's *The Corrections*, Marcus insists that Bernhard's *Correction*, "a truly difficult text," is "one of the most memorable novels I've ever read" (50). Franzen fires back by assigning Bernhard to the reading list of the novel's resident "dickhead."

In addition to being a reader of fiction, Richard is also a musician who achieves a level of artistic acclaim that leaves Walter seething with envy. His first band is a noisy, abrasive post-punk band called the Traumatics whose music would be categorized in the Status/unpopular column. Their two signature songs, "I Hate Sunshine" and "Insanely Happy," spark a Wallace-esque note. As regards the first, Franzen has argued that, though "Wallace wrote about weather as well as anyone, . . . nature itself didn't interest him" (*Farther* 37). Meanwhile, "Insanely Happy" winks playfully at *Infinite Jest*. Franzen extends these Wallace references later in the novel, when Richard and Walter attend a Bright Eyes concert. Bright Eyes, led by child prodigy Connor Oberst, traffics in an irony-free brand of earnest, hopeful folk rock, and so it is fitting that Franzen depicts the younger fans attending the concert as Wallace's children. Richard sneers at their "innocent entitlement . . . to emotion," and their repudiation of "the cynicism and anger of their elders" (369). Meanwhile, Richard views Oberst as "performing sincerity, and when the performance threatened to give sincerity the lie, he performed his sincere anguish over the difficulty of sincerity" (369–70). These last lines access Wallace's early story, "My Appearance," in which an actress about to appear on the *David Letterman Show* is warned not to appear "sincere . . . Or sincere-seeming" (*Girl* 182). Similarly, Oberst's anguished performance of "the difficulty of sincerity" recalls Wallace's own "footnotes-within-footnotes self-consciousness," as demonstrated, for instance, in the second footnote to Wallace's story "Octet," wherein the narrator breaks through the story to insist that "he's at least respectful enough of you as reader/audience to be honest about the fact that he's back there pulling strings, an 'honesty' which personally you've always had the feeling is actually a highly rhetorical sham-honesty that's designed to get you to like him and approve of him" (*Brief* 147). Earnest, naïve Walter heartily approves of Bright Eyes, insisting that its music is all about "this pantheistic effort to keep believing in something in a world full of death . . . It's like religion without the bullshit of religious dogma" (370). Here Franzen points to Wallace's indebtedness to William James's *Varieties of Religious Experience*, which informs his portrait of Alcoholics Anonymous as a secular religion.

The uncompromisingly noisy and negative Traumatics never achieve popular acclaim; by the time of their final record, Patty notes, "Richard was not having the best life; had not actually been kidding with all his self-deprecation and avowals of admiration and envy of her and Walter" (143). By this point in their friendship, Richard is a washed-up rockstar, pursuing female fans half his age, while Walter is the father of two children, a homeowner, and a successful environmentalist. But Richard eventually strikes it big when, in the late 1990s, he forms a new alt-country band called Walnut Surprise, which Franzen depicts as in the mold of Wilco, Son Volt, and the Jayhawks. After his adulterous tryst with Patty at the Berglund's Minnesota lakehouse, Nameless Lake, he records a dark, evocative record detailing his heartbreak over the event that he then names after the lake house itself. Clearly based on Bon Iver's 2007 solo album *For Emma Forever Ago*, a Nick Drake–influenced break-up record recorded, according to the liner notes, "in the burning cabin, Northwestern, Wisconsin,"[4] *Nameless Lake* earns Richard endorsements from "Michael Stipe and Jeff Tweedy," both of whom admit to having been "longtime closet Traumatic fans," before going on to become a sizeable hit with the forty-year-old NPR-listening "urban gentry" that is *Freedom*'s focus and target demographic. After Richard's immense success, Walter, Patty reveals, "became competitive" (186).

Yet their competition hardly begins here. Patty's adulterous affair with Richard at Nameless Lake culminates in a submerged but tangible struggle between the two men over Patty's affection. From the very beginning of her relationship with the two friends, Patty preferred the bad boy Richard to dogged, earnest Walter. In her autobiography, she laments, "Oh Walter: did he know that the most intriguing thing about him, in the months when Patty was

---

[4]Nickolas Butler's 2014 debut novel *Shotgun Lovesongs* also features a reclusive indie rock star who sleeps with his best friend's wife, retreats to a cabin in the north, and records an acclaimed solo acoustic album about the event.

getting to know him, was that he was Richard Katz's friend?" (75). She chooses to marry Walter only after Richard rejects her during a disastrous road trip she and Richard take in the spring of her junior year in college. Walter is not unaware of his status as his wife's runner up. When the two first attempt to sleep together, in the immediate aftermath of Richard's rebuff, Walter halts the proceedings to stammer, "Do you understand that I have a . . . a . . . [.] A problem. With Richard," before going on to explain, "I don't trust him. I love him, but I don't trust him" (128). And after their marriage, he maintains a safe distance from Richard, explaining that, in his and Richard's friendship, "he'd always felt more like the pursuer than the pursued; that there was a kind of brinkmanship between them, a competition not to be the first to blink and show need" (131). So for the next twenty years, his contact with Richard stays confined to brief overnight visits, on the rare occasions when the Traumatics roll into town.

Their close friendship gets renewed at the same moment of Patty's long deferred betrayal. In what Patty refers to as "Walter's finest hour as Richard's big brother," he offers Richard, who, after the demise of the Traumatics, loses his apartment, the opportunity to live rent free at Nameless Lake (153). Somewhat improbably, Walter leaves Patty and Richard alone at the lake, during which weekend Patty, a lifelong nonreader, completes *War and Peace*. Tolstoy's epic novel serves as another clue linking Richard's betrayal to Wallace. *War and Peace* itself summons *Infinite Jest* in its size, scope, and prominence, while the depiction of Patty raptly reading the book playfully taps into Franzen's and Wallace's directives for the power of fiction to, as Franzen puts it in his first eulogy to Wallace, "create that 'neutral middle ground on which to make a deep connection with another human being'" (*Farther* 164). Patty admits she might have resisted sleeping with Richard, even after all that history, "if she hadn't reached the final pages in which Natasha Rostov, who was obviously meant for goofy and good Pierre, falls in love with his great cool friend, Prince Andrei" (166). Patty obviously conflates Andrei with Richard and Walter with Pierre—later she refers to Walter as "her own Pierre"—an autobiographical projection that knocks down the last of her meager defenses (175). In short, while reading *War and Peace*, she ends up making a deep connection with another human being; unfortunately, that human being is not Tolstoy, but Richard.

Meanwhile, Patty hardly ignores *War and Peace*'s "military stuff," which she admits absorbed her as much as the novel's love triangle (166). Here Franzen playfully associates Walter's cuckolding with Napoleon's defeat. Before he leaves the two of them in the lake house, Walter plays chess with Richard while Patty sits in her mother-in-law's "favorite armchair, reading *War and Peace*" (156). As the two men struggle to capture each other's queen—Patty, in this reading—Patty grafts her own situation onto that of Natasha Rostov, whose struggle to choose between Pierre and Andrei takes place against the backdrop of chess's real life model, actual war. Franzen has written about "the awkward chess games" he and Wallace played together, and so the chess here serves as one more detail linking Walter and Richard's romantic rivalry to Franzen and Wallace's literary competition. (*Farther* 165). Patty notes with relief that "Walter was better than Richard at chess and usually won" (156). Conversely, after her second bout of sex with Richard, which event marks for her "the first time she'd properly had sex," she tells Richard, "You may suck at chess, . . . but you're definitely winning at the other game" (169, 170). Walter's superior strategic thinking is no match for Richard's sexual charisma.

Yet for all of its bitterness, Walter and Richard's friendship is grounded in what the cynical Richard admits is "something that insists on being called love" (205). The word "love" is in fact Franzen's key single-entendre principal. In his Kenyon Commencement Address, Franzen pits "actual love" of another human being against the "narcissistic tendencies of technology" (*Farther* 8). He argues that love is "always specific," and that "to love a specific person, and to identify with their struggles and joys as if they were your own, you have to surrender some of yourself" (*Farther* 9). Conversely, in "Farther Away" he marks the "near perfect absence" in Wallace's fiction of "ordinary love" (39). What's more, in *Freedom*, Franzen situates love as the obverse of freedom writ large. "Love of a specific person" provides his characters with purpose and meaning even as it robs them of their independence; freedom, on the other hand, while preserving his characters' autonomy, leaves them trapped on their own islands. Walter's love of Patty and Richard binds him and hems him in, while their son Joey's radical demand for total freedom is ultimately undercut by "an ache named Connie at the center of his life" (408).

Late in her life, Patty observes that "few circumstances have turned out to be more painful to the autobiographer, in the long run, than the dearness of Walter and Richard's friendship" (66). She also notes that both men are "struggling, albeit in different ways, to be good people." That last phrase, repeated throughout the book, is also the title of a short excerpt from *The Pale King* that Wallace published in the *New Yorker*. For his part, Walter is "tormented by the suspicion that he loved Richard more than Richard loved him" (135). And, as we have seen, Richard, too, regards his deepest feelings for Walter as resembling "something" like love. In fact, his friendship with Walter is the only stable relationship in his life, particularly since, as Patty notes, "Richard had no relationship with his mom" (133). Walter is not only a beloved brother for Richard but also the embodiment of what he lacks. At one point Richard calls Walter his "conscience" (204). His "strong (if highly intermittent) wish to be a good person" drives him repeatedly back into the bosom of the Berglund family, where he can bask in not only Walter's goodness but also that of their idealistic daughter Jessica, to whom he listens with what Walter regards as the "fake and condescending" attentiveness that Richard reserves only for those "whom he considered Good" (133–34). Patty dismisses Walter's critique under the assumption that Walter, even here, "was in competition with him" and considered "the province of listening to women with sincere attentiveness [was] most definitely *his* turf" (134). Here Franzen might be touching upon Wallace's habit of listening closely to women, which, as D. T. Max suggests, was one of Wallace's key seductive techniques. As touched upon in the Eugenides chapter, Max argues that Wallace's "dedication—sexily flawed—to what might be called single-entendre connections was extremely intoxicating to some woman" (233). Accordingly, again as noted previously, Eugenides depicts Leonard at one point as "staring into a girl's face as if attempting a mind-meld" (92), while his lover Madeleine observes that she had "never met anyone, and certainly not a guy, who was so receptive, who took everything in . . . Whenever she was with him, Leonard gave her his full attention" (92, 61).

In a final overlap with *The Marriage Plot*, Franzen frames Richard and Walter's love within the contours of Eve Sedgwick's *Between Men*. As briefly explored earlier, Sedgwick builds upon René Girard's *Deceit, Desire, and the Novel*, wherein Girard explores a number of fictionalized love triangles in which two men compete for the affection of a female. According to Sedgwick, "It is the bond between males that he most assiduously uncovers" (21). She goes on to argue that this bond, usually figured as only "homosocial," should in fact be seen as operating on "the potential unbrokenness of a continuum between homosocial and homosexual—a continuum whose visibility, for men, in our society, is radically disrupted" (2–3). She chooses to regard the bond between the men as grounded in "desire" rather than merely "love" to "mark the erotic emphasis" (3). She employs the term "'desire' in a way analogous to the psychoanalytic use of 'libido'—not for a particular affective state of emotion, but for the affective social force, the glue, even when its manifestation is hostility or hatred or something less emotively charged" (3).

Franzen is overt about the erotic desire lurking beneath the brotherly love between Richard and Walter. Early on, Eliza, noting Walter's possessive hatred of her, wonders if "he's really jealous of me. I think he's got some kind of thing for Richard. Maybe a gay thing" (75). Similarly, Patty notes that, as with herself, "Walter claimed to have loved Richard at first sight" (131). Richard, too, cannot separate his love for Walter from desire. His friendship is complicated, he realizes, by his "being no less attracted to Patty than Walter was, and arguably *more* attracted to Walter than Patty was" (205). Furthermore, he realizes that "no other man had warmed Katz's loins the way the sight of Walter did after long absence" (205). And although he insists these "groinal heatings were no more about literal sex, no more homo, than the hard-ons he got from a long-anticipated first snort of blow, . . . there was definitely something deep-chemical there" (205). Finally, in the most direct nod to Sedgwick, Richard admits that "he wanted Walter's women not in spite of his friendship but because of it" (208). Late in the novel, Patty echoes Richard's assessment when she realizes that "nothing between Patty and Richard was ever going to last, . . . because neither was as loveable to the other as Walter was to both of them," and that, in loving Richard, "she was actually loving Walter" (509, 510). In other words, Patty, Richard, and Walter's shared object of desire is merely the means by which they work out the "radically disrupted" desire they feel for each other. Given that Franzen has gone to great lengths to equate Richard with his penis, and his sexual prowess with Wallace's literary same, their competition for Patty grafts neatly onto the Franzen/Wallace literary rivalry. Wallace, the self-involved literary rockstar, cuckolds the more staid writer of doggedly realistic domestic novels such as *The Corrections* and *Freedom*. Or, to reverse Marcus's diagnosis, Mr. Difficult covets what Mr. Contract possesses. For all of that, the rivalry is underwritten by love.

The subplot involving Walter's son Joey provides further confirmation of Franzen's debt to Sedgwick. Like his father, Joey, too, is involved in a love triangle. What's more, his male rival is also his college roommate, a boy named, not coincidentally, *Jonathan*. In this triangle, however, Joey desires Jonathan's shallow, rich sister, Jenna, while Jonathan, Franzen makes all too clear, desires Joey. Throughout their friendship, Jonathan makes thinly veiled gay slurs at Joey, as when he notes the lingering smell of semen following one of Joey's many masturbation sessions and says, "I mean, I like you and all, but I'm not ready to go all the way yet" (258). Similarly, his usual nickname for Joey is "pretty boy" (264). Late in their relationship, noting how betrayed Jonathan feels about Joey's single-minded pursuit of his sister, Joey asks if Jonathan hates him, to which Jonathan replies, "I think you've been a total asshole. But hating you doesn't seem to be an option for me" (438). In this scenario, Jonathan occupies the Walter/Franzen role. Jonathan even echoes Walter's political opinions regarding the Iraq War. Both he and Jonathan "enjoyed reversing their expected roles and becoming the political outliers of their respective families, Joey sounding more and more like Jonathan's father, Jonathan more and more like Joey's" (394). Joey by extension functions as a stand-in for Richard, a connection strengthened by Franzen's repeated references to Joey and his sexual organ. At one key moment, Joey, masturbating yet again, fondly regards his erection's "independence" and its "repulsive beauty" and notes ruefully that to "walk around hard every minute of the day . . . would be to be what people called a prick" (251). Nevertheless, Jonathan flat out calls Joey "a dick" (401).

Joey's story does not merely repeat his father's, however, because of the presence of a fourth person, namely Connie, Joey's childhood love. For Jonathan, Connie, rather than Jenna, serves as the displaced means by which he can express his desire for Joey. Jonathan, who "had no sex life," was "terminally awkward with girls, awkward to the point of not being interested," whereas with Connie, "he could relax and be himself" (391). He heartily champions Joey's relationship with Connie, whom he thinks is *"amazing,* totally hot but also easy to be with" (391). As Joey continues to betray Connie by pursuing Jenna, Jonathan severely criticizes Joey "as if he were Connie's older brother or knightly guardian" (401). Ultimately, Jonathan calls Joey a "dick and a liar, unworthy of Connie," (401). Jonathan's language directly echoes that of Richard, who tells Patty, "I thought you were a person who was actually worthy of Walter" (172).

But despite his best efforts, Joey cannot shake Connie. For Bergström, Connie is the "(m)Other figure that Joey's default self does not *choose* to feel an obligation to; he just does" (126). He marries her on what he imagines is a whim, nevertheless noting that the walk to the judge's office "felt as long as his entire life before it" (417). Similarly, he regards his wedding ring as "his soul, his familiar personal self" (390). In an essay that reads the novel in the context of the 9/11 tragedy, Paul Jenner correctly observes, "Somewhat inconveniently and, in literary critical terms, unfashionably, Franzen has Joey discover something approaching a core self and personality" (169). In a grisly comic chain of events, Joey accidentally swallows the ring and, while on a disastrous weekend away with Jenna, has to sift through his own feces to recover it. Franzen associates the feces with Joey's avaricious, capitalist drive for wealth—filthy lucre and so on—whereby his separating the ring from his shit constitutes his recovering his "soul" amid his love of money. Franzen confirms this reading when he has Joey realize that he

> was being driven crazy by so minutely feeling what [Connie] felt, by understanding her too well, by not being able to imagine his life without her. Every time he had a chance to get away from her, the logic of self-interest failed him: was supplanted, like a gear that his mind kept popping out of, by the logic of the two of them. (409)

Love defeats freedom. The capitalist doctrine of "self-interest" proves unequal to the love of a specific person. In his conclusion to "Farther Away," Franzen echoes this sentiment when he observes that Defoe, in his portrait of Crusoe, "gave us the first realistic portrait of the radically isolated individual, and then, as if impelled by novelistic truth, he showed us how sick and crazy radical individualism really is" (52). In a novel steeped with richly evocative names, it is no accident that Patty's self-absorbed father is named Emerson, the father of American self-reliance. Walter, a sort of anti-Joey, reverses his son's experience with his wedding ring when, after he and Patty separate, he flushes his ring down the toilet (408). Temporarily freed of his matrimonial bond, Walter crusades for birds. At one level, his effort to protect the birds provides a way for him to mourn the death of his lover, Lalitha, who tragically dies in a car accident and whom Walter conflates with "dead songbirds in the wild—they were impossibly light to begin with, and as soon as their little hearts stopped beating they were barely more than bits of fluff and hollow bone" (555). Similarly, the neighborhood's population of feral cats, who pose such a threat to the birds, serve as the subliminal targets for his rage at Richard. Throughout the text, Franzen invites us to conflate Katz with cats.[5] In a scene midway through the novel, for instance, Walter thinks he hears Lalitha, say, "It's like the problem with Katz," to which Richard himself replies, "Moi?": "Kitty cats," she clarifies, before cataloging her and Walter's objection to these allegedly benign bird murderers (222). Richard also consistently refers to all of his female conquests, Patty includes, as "chicks" (555). Cats, Walter notes, "were all about using people" (550). It is also no accident that the local cat who most focuses Walter's transferred rage is named Bobby, for Franzen also relates Richard to Bob Dylan. Richard considers Dylan to be "an asshole, the beautifully pure kind of asshole who made a younger musician want to be an asshole himself" (132). Patty observes that the Dylan documentary *Don't Look Back* is "a touchstone for both Richard and Walter" (134). The scene in the movie that stands out for Patty is one in which Dylan outshines Donovan. Although she notes that "Walter felt sorry for Donovan—and, what's more, felt bad about himself for not wanting to be more like Dylan and less like Donovan," Patty finds thrilling "the breathtaking nakedness of

---

[5]When he was asked by an audience member on the Oprah Winfrey show if the name of his character Richard Katz was intentionally designed to link the character to domestic *cats*, since Richard is "predatory like a cat, and Walter hates cats," Franzen nervously replied, "That was just another . . . that's another great question, a terrific question," and then falls silent for comic moment or two, suggesting that he would rather not answer. Ultimately, he *doesn't* answer her question, merely suggesting that the name "just happened" ("Jonathan Franzen on the Naming of Richard Katz"). Franzen's nonresponse affirms that the questioner already *has* her answer.

Dylan's competitiveness" and comes to understand "why Richard preferred to hang out with the unmusical Walter, rather than the hipsters" (134–35). Eventually, Walter deposits Bobby at an animal shelter "that would either kill it or fob it off on an urban family" (549). The errand fails to satisfy him, however, for he recognizes that "he and Bobby had in some way been married to each other, and that even a horrible marriage was less lonely than no marriage at all" (550). Sustaining the parallel between Bobby and Richard, he also notes that "the small animal vulnerability in Bobby's face made him aware of the fatal defect in his own makeup, the defect of pitying even the beings he most hated" (551).

Right on cue, Patty returns to Walter, waiting out in the cold so that he must carry her back inside and revive her by clutching her body to his until his own animal warmth brings her back to life. The hatred he feels for her, and for Richard, is impossible to separate from the abiding love that underscores all. To love a specific person, Franzen argues in his Kenyon address, opens up the risk of rejection, which can be "catastrophically painful," but he insists that "pain hurts, but it doesn't kill," and to go through life "painless is not to have lived" (11). Walter, having brought Patty back to life, stares into her eye to let her "see all the vileness inside him, all the hatreds of two thousand solitary nights, while the two of them were still in touch with the void in which the sum of everything they'd ever said or done, every pain they'd inflicted, every joy they'd shared, would weigh less than the smallest figure on the wind" (559).

This final valediction, inspired in part by his inability to dispense entirely with the specter of Bobby, also applies, by default, to Richard. And here we arrive at the most important component of Franzen's complex, fictionalized allegory for his relationship with his own brother, friend, and rival, David Foster Wallace. On one level, it is hard to avoid the assessment that *Freedom* mounts a scandalously harsh indictment of that friendship. But, as Franzen spells out with painful lucidity in *Farther Away*, suicide represents a special case. One has every right to feel anger and revengeful rage against the murderer of one's beloved friend; the problem with suicide is that the murderer *is* the beloved friend. Franzen seems to express some form of this sentiment when, as noted earlier, he describes his feelings following Wallace's death as consisting of "fleeting grief and enduring anger" (20). But he provides a more pertinent response to unfair charges of emotional disregard in his 2009 essay, "On Autobiographical Fiction." First, he reveals that, in writing *Freedom*, he found a new literary ally in our most disruptive and transgressive writer of autobiographical fiction, Philip Roth, finding his scabrous *Sabbath's Theater* in particular to be a "correction and reproach of the sentimentality of certain young American writers and not-so-young critics who seem to believe . . . that literature is about being nice" (125).[6] More importantly, he recounts his struggle, while writing *The Corrections*, to square his loyalty to his brother with his need to write a character based largely on him. He wonders how he "could use details from [his brother's] life without hurting him and jeopardizing [their] good relations" (139). He then reasons, "All loyalties, both in writing and elsewhere, are meaningful only when they're tested" (139). He then argues

> there's potential value, not only for your writing but also for your relationships, in taking autobiographical risks: that you may, in fact, be doing your brother or your mother or *your best friend* a favor by giving them the opportunity to rise to the occasion of being written about—by trusting them to love the whole you. (140, emphasis added)

The two important points for Franzen are that the writer "write as truthfully as possible," and that, if the writer "really love[s] the person whose material [he's] writing about, the writing reflects that love" (140).

Writers of novels are under no obligation to affirm or refute the readings critics or casual readers might impose on their novels. Nor are they even obliged to be conscious of the intricate connections that lurk beneath the text's dense, metaphorical texture, connections that resemble the connections underlying a dream. Franzen himself, while describing *how* his fiction is autobiographical, asks, "What is fiction, after all, if not a kind of purposeful dreaming? The writer works to create a dream that is vivid and has meaning, so that the reader can then vividly dream it and experience meaning" (*Farther* 129). *Freedom* comes nowhere near to being a *roman à clef*, and, aside from a few concrete particulars—Richard's dipping,

---

[6]Another possible component in Franzen's late appreciation for Roth might be found on the back jacket of the hardcover edition of *Farther Away*, which features the following blurb from Roth: "There are about twenty great American novelists in the generations that follow me. The greatest is Jonathan Franzen."

his and Walter's chess games—the novel does not fictionalize actual
scenes from the author's friendship with his rival. Rather, it does
something more interesting. In fact, *interesting* is a key word in the
novel, repeated nearly a dozen times and applied over and over
again to various characters, Patty in particular (see for instance
95, 217, 228). Franzen's repeated use of the word calls to mind
Henry James's famous dictum, "The only obligation to which in
advance we hold a novel, without incurring the accusation of being
arbitrary, is that it be interesting" ("Art of Fiction" 349).[7] In this
regard, *Freedom* works not as a work of autobiography but rather
as a work of fiction grounded in an honest confrontation with the
writer's own life and an unrelenting desire to honor James's cardinal
rule. As Franzen argues, the "greater autobiographical content" of
a novel often has very little "resemblance to the writer's actual life"
(*Farther* 129). In fact, he insists that the "deeper the writer digs for
meaning, the more the random particulars of the writer's life become
impediments to deliberate dreaming" (*Farther* 129). The dream is
what prevails, and, in the case of *Freedom,* that dream, for all the
pain it discloses, is both truthful and loving. To give James the final
word, "There is . . . no more nutritive or suggestive truth in this
connexion than that of the perfect dependence of the 'moral' sense
of a work of art on the amount of felt life concerned in producing
it" ("Preface" ix–x).

---

[7]Here, too, Franzen might be drawing upon Roth, who engaged in a career-long
dialogue with the Master, beginning with *Letting Go*'s intricate echoes of *Portrait
of a Lady* and continuing with Zuckerman's numerous invocations of James's work
and criticism. *The Counterlife* in particular makes repeated references to James's
dictum about the need for a novel to be "interesting." In the first section, which
records his brother Henry's death, he wonders if his brother's conventional wife is
"a more interesting woman than he'd thought" (48). He wonders the same thing
about Henry in the subsequent chapter, when Henry, now very much alive, moves to
Israel to get in touch with his authentic Jewish identity: "What if Henry has signed
on with the Jewish cause without believing a word? Could he have become that
interesting?" (120). Later, Zuckerman reveals what being "interesting" really means
for a novelist like himself: "People don't turn themselves over to writers as full-blown
literary characters—generally they give you very little to go on, and after the initial
impression, are barely any help at all. Most people (beginning with the novelist—
himself, his family, just about everyone he knows) are absolutely unoriginal, and his
job is to make them appear otherwise . . . If Henry was ever going to turn out to be
interesting, I was going to have to do it" (156).

6

Against Wallace

Amy Hungerford, Lauren Groff, and the Resistance to Genius

An Internet literary genre is being born. Call it Wallace Snark. Although there are numerous variations on the form, the genre, generally speaking, consists of literary blogs by women complaining about their boyfriends and, by extension, David Foster Wallace. The tone ranges from *Onion*-esque sarcasm to unfiltered anger, but the collective resentment of Wallace—or, more specifically, of his doorstop novel *Infinite Jest*—remains consistent, however sardonically the resentment is expressed. Dierdre Coyle wastes no time in declaring her intent in her blog entry, "Men Recommend David Foster Wallace to Me." She opens the piece with the following one-two punch: "For a while, I was seeing a guy who really liked David Foster Wallace. He once forced me to do cocaine by shoving it inside me during sex. He wasn't the first man to recommend Wallace, but he's the last whose suggestion I pretended to consider. So while I've never read a book by Wallace, I'm preemptively uninterested in your opinion about it." Jessye McGarry's "Why I'm Waiting for the Right Man to Tell Me I Should Read *Infinite*

Jest" represents the genre at its snarkiest. Presented as a parody of a women's-magazine dating confession, McGarry observes, "As a woman in the dating world, I'm constantly trying to find the right man to spend the rest of my life with. So many people ask me when I'm going to settle down and have someone tell me to read David Foster Wallace's *Infinite Jest*." In both cases, the implication is the same: boys who ask their girlfriends to read David Foster Wallace are controlling jerks.

Such is the overt thesis of Molly Fischer's much quoted 2015 column in *New York Magazine*'s The Cut feature, wherein she deems Wallace the patron saint of "literary chauvinists" or, as she calls them later in the piece, "lit-bros." She relays a story told by a female acquaintance about a "bookish male acquaintance with a man-bun." "That guy," Fischer quotes her friend as saying, "I just feel like he's *first* in line to see the David Foster Wallace movie," by which she means *The End of the Tour*, starring Jason Seigel as a bandana-capped Wallace. For his part, Seigel recalls purchasing a copy of *Infinite Jest* as part of his research for playing the author, whereupon the young woman behind the bookstore counter remarked, "Every guy I've ever dated has an unread copy on his bookshelf." As Fischer ruefully admits, all of these stories mine "a familiar vein" (Fischer).

Another unavoidable takeaway from these essays—and there are many more out there—is that the authors by and large have not actually read *Infinite Jest*. As Jonathan Russell Clark points out in his riposte to Fischer, "Reclaiming David Foster Wallace from the Lit-Bros," although Fischer is careful to point out that the particular "lit-bros" she's complaining about have never read *Infinite Jest*, neither, it would seem, has she: "In her essay she quotes from Adelle Waldman's *The Love Affairs of Nathaniel P.* and Heidi Julavits' *The Folded Clock*, but never from *Infinite Jest*" (Clark). This failure—or, as we shall see, pointed refusal—to address the book itself is also one of the key features of the genre, and of the complaint. The lit-bros urging their lovers to read Wallace are guilty for the mere act of recommending the book in the first place. The recommendation represents an affront, if not a sexist act of aggression. Refusing to read the book has become an act of resistance.

That resistance has also occasioned a number of baroque and recondite variations on the Wallace/Lit-Bro genre. The most curious is the case of comedian Jamie Loftis, who, as part of an extended performance art piece, has spent a year quite literally *eating Infinite Jest*, page by page. Fans of Loftis's piece can go to *#eatinginfinitejest* to watch videos of her eating pages of the novel in the form of sandwiches or paperballs. Clayton Purdham, in a brief article about Loftis posted at A. V. Club, argues that Loftis's piece "seems engineered to enrage the book's acolytes," particularly given that, throughout her videos, she repeatedly makes the point "of displaying her total ignorance of" the novel itself (Purdham). Similarly, Mira Gonzales turned her unread copy of *Infinite Jest* into a bong and smoked marijuana from it, arguing, "I will not take time out of my only life to read a footnoted book that is 1,079 pages long. I refuse" (Gonzales). Here, the book itself, the physical object, is the affront that must be desecrated. In keeping with the genre, the authors boldly and unequivocally base their assessment of the book's worth, or lack thereof, on the lit-bros they know who have read it, and who seem especially committed to it. As in the Seigel episode, Loftis tells Gonzales that her decision to eat, rather than read, the novel resulted from her experience working as a bookstore clerk. She declares that "every chode who came into the bookstore I worked at would buy [*Infinite Jest*] and unhinge their jaw to scold me when I said I hadn't read it myself . . . It appears to be a status symbol in the chode community" (Gonzales). Although a "chode" technically refers to a penis that is wider than it is long, Loftis airily insists that, for her anyway, the word refers to "pseudo-intellectuals"—and, in all fairness, it does not require a huge leap of the imagination to see how she arrived at this functional shift. One is reminded, unavoidably, of Wallace's own reference to John Updike as "a penis with a thesaurus."

This is all very cute but hardly edifying. Much more serious, though no less problematic, is scholar Amy Hungerford's strident argument against reading *Infinite Jest*, first excerpted in *The Chronicle of Higher Education* as "On Not Reading" before it reappeared as "On Not Reading DFW" in her recent monograph, *Making Literature*. A professor of English and dean of the Humanities Division at Yale University, Hungerford is a major scholar of contemporary US fiction; her works include *Postmodern Belief: American Literature and Religion since 1960* (Princeton University Press, 2010) and *The Holocaust of Texts: Genocide Literature and Personification* (University of Chicago Press, 2003). She has written on various religious strains in the work of Don

DeLillo and Jonathan Safron Foer, both key figures in the Wallace literary orbit, and so her refusal to read *Infinite Jest* carries with it an aura of scholarly gravitas that distinguishes it from the snarky blogs already addressed. Notice must be taken.

She divides her argument into three components. First, she begins with the commonplace observation that there is simply too much to read these days, a particularly vexing situation for a scholar of contemporary fiction, who, like Hungerford, must make careful determinations regarding how she allots her limited professional reading time. As she argues, "Nonreading, seen in this light, is not a badge of shame, but the way of the future" (Hungerford). She next addresses the already existing mechanism by which reading choices in the academy are reduced to a manageable level, namely canonization. While she grants that the "Restoration-era scholar" is "aided by generations of readers who have studied [Pope's] works . . . and presented [edited] collections of them," she insists that, for the scholar of contemporary literature, canonization cannot be trusted. For one thing, canonization in the case of contemporary fiction is replaced by the vagaries of "the literary market," which "as a whole is vulnerable to forces that have less to do with literary discernment and more to do with money, class, contemporary pressures on journalists, the geographies of cities, and the social networks that circumscribe the reach of editorial attention or a bookstore's clientele" (Hungerford). But she equally distrusts the canonization that has winnowed out the modernist and early postmodern corpus. She cites a 1987 essay by Richard Ohmann addressing the reception of J. D. Salinger's *Catcher in the Rye*, in which Ohmann sets contemporary reviews of Salinger's novel "next to the constellation of advertisements that surrounded the review . . . tracking the lines of connection between the publishers' buying space and the appearance of a review." Hungerford then endorses Ohmann's conclusion that Salinger's "pungent class critique and . . . implicit call to think collectively" have ever since been "submerged" by the initial reviewers' insistence on reading the novel as "mourning conformity and our compromised liberal self-determination," a reading, Ohmann suggests, that was imposed upon the novel by the conflation of postwar jingoism and the publisher's original promotional push. Similarly, she cites a talk by Andrew Goldstone given at the 2014 meeting of the Modern Language Association in which Goldstone inventoried the literary figures addressed most often in the journal *Modernism/modernity* over a twenty-year period. He concluded that "a handful of major canonical authors—Joyce, Woolf, Eliot, Stein, Beckett, etc"— claimed 41 percent of the articles, while "most authors not already canonical appear only once or twice, never achieving the critical mass of scholarship that motivates further study" (Hungerford). The system of canonization, in other words, favors the canonical.

These key points set up her argument for not reading the work of David Foster Wallace. In sum, Wallace's work takes too long to read, and his prominence obscures other writers worthy of our attention. She complains not only that "the machine of his celebrity masks . . . the limited benefits of spending the time to read his work" but also that Little, Brown's initial marketing campaign for *Infinite Jest* "appealed to a Jurassic vision of literary genius" that she rejects. Finally, she takes great offense at an observation Wallace made to his editor, Michael Pietsch, that the novel's "length and obscurities" were justified because "he expected people to read it twice" (Hungerford).

I have outlined the argument at such length because I wish to do it justice. Even so, this writer is left scratching his head. At the simplest level, one can object that Hungerford is not in a position to argue for the "limited benefits" of reading a book she has not read. As Christopher Hitchens was wont to say, that which can be asserted without evidence can be dismissed without evidence. "The machine of his celebrity" is not evidence against the book, though it might be evidence against his celebrity. But Hungerford's other claims also wobble under scrutiny. To the charge that there is simply too much to read, it is perhaps worth noting that this is ever the case. Samuel Johnson made the exact same complaint in 1753, adding, "It may be observed that, of this, as of other evils, complaints have been made by every generation" (Johnson 284). But Hungerford also never entertains the possibility that more people write about Joyce and Woolf because Joyce and Woolf are simply more worth writing about, or that their works are so uniquely dense and resilient, not to mention emotionally and intellectual resonant, that they encourage and withstand close and repeated attention, which are the very hallmarks of literary excellence, after all. Her rejection of Wallace's work on the basis of the "machinery of his celebrity" also fails to note that *Infinite Jest* was largely ignored by the literary establishment that would have been the first agent in

the novel's canonization. It neither won nor was even shortlisted
for a single major literary prize—not the National Book Award,
not the National Book Critics Circle Award, not the Pulitzer Prize.
If book reviewers and contemporary tastemakers cannot be trusted
with the task of determining what we should read, as Hungerford
argues, then *Infinite Jest* could just as easily be marked as a work
that overcame that initial winnowing effort.[1] What's more the first
serious scholarship on Wallace's work appeared in 2003, nearly a
decade after the publication of *Infinite Jest*, and so it is a stretch
to attribute the widespread interest in Wallace's work, and the rise
of "Wallace studies" more generally, to "a particular marketing
campaign" issued in 1996 and which resulted in the book's being
totally ignored by the key gatekeepers of literary taste. In other
words, it is quite possible that the predominance of Wallace's novel
in contemporary literary scholarship might have something to do
with the novel itself, a claim Hungerford could confirm or refute
simply by reading it.

What seems to infuriate Hungerford the most, and which
I suspect drives her refusal to confront *Infinite Jest* directly, is
exactly that "Jurassic vision of literary genius" that Wallace's major
novel invokes, and which Wallace overtly courted. As I have charted
throughout this study, Wallace positioned himself, and *Infinite Jest*,
as the culmination of a trajectory of literary experimentation and
high achievement that is resolutely white, male, and exclusive.
Wallace's major novel further fulfilled a contract of not just length
and density but also difficulty and forbiddingness that begins with
the example of *Moby-Dick* and continues through Joyce's *Ulysses*,
Gaddis's *The Recognitions*, and Pynchon's *Gravity's Rainbow*.
For many scholars of contemporary literature, this vertical, male
trajectory represents a "Jurassic vision of literary genius" that has
been supplanted by a more democratic vision of multicultural

---

[1] The 1996 National Book Award went to Andrea Barrett's *Ship Fever and Other Stories*. The NBA finalists included Ron Hansen's *Atticus*, Elizabeth McCracken's *The Giant's House*, Steven Millhauser's *Martin Dressler: The Tale of an American Dreamer*, and Janet Peery's *The River beyond the World*. The 1996 National Book Critics Circle Award went to Gina Berriault's *Women in Their Beds*; the finalists were Louis Begley's *About Schmidt*, Andre Dubus's *Dancing after Hours*, Jamaica Kincaid's *The Autobiography of My Mother*, and Henry Roth's *From Bondage*. Richard Ford's *Independence Day* won the 1996 Pulitzer Prize for Fiction.

literary production focused on difference, diversity, and a horizontal embrace of marginalized voices.

But Hungerford does not level these reasonable objections. Rather, her complaint lies with Wallace's audacity in writing a book that takes a month to read—a month that would be better spent, Hungerford argues, reading four other novels. To the objection that millions of readers have in fact spent that required month with the book and emerged as enthusiastic advocates, Hungerford counters that such readers have been duped. The book's initial readers, she argues, "having committed the time, . . . had then to prove, in writing, that they had something equally smart to say about it" (Hungerford). All subsequent readers have fallen for the same ruse such that the book's current stature is the produce of "the self-perpetuating machine of literary celebrity." Her abiding point is that *there is no there*: of this she is "absolutely sure [she is] right" (Hungerford).

Hungerford's essay as well as Loftis's online stunt of eating *Infinite Jest* and Gonzales's transformation of her copy into a bong all signal the degree to which Wallace's novel is now regarded as a grim obligation for people who are committed to contemporary cultural literacy. It is no longer enough simply to refuse to read the book, for such refusal now carries with it an implicit charge of weakness and inadequacy, a charge made all the more galling not only by Wallace's hulking masculinity—the whole bandana-wearing-nerd-bro image perpetuated by the machinery of his celebrity—but also by the overwhelmingly maleness of his readership. For female readers, Hungerford suggests, being urged to read the novel is tantamount to being challenged to a test of strength and stamina. In her view, that initial Little, Brown marketing campaign, which she credits with establishing the novel's undeserved stature, could be reduced to the following question: "Are you smart enough and strong enough—indeed, are you man enough—to read a genius's thousand-page novel?" (Hungerford). In this atmosphere, it is understandable why so many would-be readers are compelled, both figuratively and literally, to hollow out the book, to scrape out its mass and density and leave it desiccated and deflated.

What is perhaps most disappointing about this last aspect of the current wave of resentment for *Infinite Jest* is how divorced it is from the actual experience of reading the book. Although stamina is no doubt required, that stamina takes the form of a monastic form of intense, silent concentration. What Wallace asks of his readers is for them to turn off their phones and laptops, their hi-fis and streaming devices, and undertake a process of reading that is offered as a balm for the decentering distractions of the information age. Millions of readers have undergone this process and have emerged from it transformed. For people who have not read the book, the pious testimonials of those who have "been there" also contribute, I would submit, to the resentment the book has inspired. The Wallace "scolds" Loftis noted are of a piece with other sanctimonious new converts to some arduous "life-changing" experience: *I just spent a week at a meditative retreat and you must do the same.* As with other such scolds, the claims made seem to the unconvinced inflated and naïve. But that aspect of the *Infinite Jest* reading experience, while it has generated the current push back, is also the source of the book's continuing popularity and cultural significance, to the understandable annoyance of nonreaders.

In my capacity as a Wallace scholar, I encounter those new converts on a regular basis. About once or twice a year, I will exit my office en route to a class or a committee meeting and find a student I have never met before sitting nervously in the chair outside my office door. The student will be hunched over a worn copy of *Infinite Jest*. These recent arrivals from "that farthest-away island which was David," to reprise Franzen's figure, have read the novel on their own, often over the summer, and the experience has left them shaken (*Farther* 39). They simply want to talk about it. Usually, they often tell me that no one in their immediate circle has read the book, and I often sense that they have long since exhausted their friends' patience on the subject of *Infinite Jest*. But the desire to connect with other visitors to Wallace Island persists. They often ask to audit my biannual *Infinite Jest* Senior Seminar to give them an excuse to read the book a second time. In fact, in the days before I began drafting this essay, a new staff member at my college charged with handling the College's accreditation assessment knocked on my door and introduced himself. For the past several years, he has been looking for someone, anyone, with whom to discuss *Infinite Jest*, which he's read five times. In twenty years of teaching twentieth-century US literature, *Infinite Jest* is the only novel that has compelled perfect strangers to lurk outside my door.

A complex form of this same brand of "lit-bro" resentment informs novelist Lauren Groff's acclaimed 2015 bestseller, *Fates and Furies*.

In her case, that aura of resentment—the "fury" in her two-part title—encompasses larger questions about female creativity, white male privilege, and the mysterious, subterranean ways power manifests itself. While the novel engages with Wallace in much more oblique and subtle ways than do the other texts in this study, her portrait of a competitive creative partnership, in this case a marriage, places her whirlwind novel in fascinating dialogue with *The Marriage Plot* and *Freedom*, specifically.

Groff shares Wallace's alma mater, Amherst College, from which she was graduated with a double major in French and English (creative writing). What's more, in interviews, she has spoken favorably of Wallace and his work. In an online interview with Brad Listi for his blog "OTHERPPL," conducted while she was writing of *Fates and Furies*, Listi asks her if Wallace "loomed large" in campus writing circles and in her mind. She replies, "He was *enor*mous!" (Listi). She also reveals that she read *Infinite Jest* during her senior year Spring Break. Earlier in the same interview, she discusses her ongoing project of rereading Great Works with an eye toward reassessment. Of the works she has read so far, she lists Herman Melville's *Moby-Dick*, Vladimir Nabokov's *Lolita*, and Marcel Proust's *In Search of Lost Time*, all of which blueprint the "Jurassic vision of literary genius" that Wallace sought to embody and which Hungerford rejects. It is perhaps no accident that all three works have left their trace in the dense, exhilarating web of allusions and intertextual play that is the surging undercurrent of *Fates and Furies*' searing domestic drama.

The book's "literary genius" is a playwright named Lancelot Satterwhite, whose parents, Gawain and Antoinette, bear equally mythical names. For most of the novel he goes by his nickname, Lotto, which is fitting since his story is told in the first section, titled "Fates." As Robin Black observes in her favorable *New York Times* review, although his nickname signals Lotto's "link to such chance-related activities as lotteries," it even more importantly speaks to his good luck (1). From the very beginning Groff describes him as "vivid: a light flickered in him that caught the eye and held it" (3), while Black notes a moment early in the novel in which Groff's intrusive narrator observes, "For now, he's the one we can't look away from. He's the shining one" (5). At the same time, his "luck" is inseparable from the privilege he enjoys as a tall, rich, white male. That privilege also gets a hand from the many women who work behind the scenes to make him a success, a list that includes his mother, his remarkable wife Mathilde, and even Groff herself. Early on, his mother realizes that "if he was going to be a great man, which he was, she was certain, she would start his greatness now" (11). After his postcollege marriage, his wife Mathilde steers his career as a playwright, not only looking after all business matters but also editing and revising his plays and quietly plotting to secure productions. "All the strings led to Mathilde's pointed finger," the narrator reveals, "and she moved it with the subtlest twitches and made [Lotto] dance" (61). All the while, Groff, the novel's Prospero, guides both characters and the plot itself to make Lancelot successful while also slyly dismantling the same vision of male literary greatness that Lotto embodies. While Lotto is still in prep school, the narrator observes, "Luck was on his side," at which point Groff's narrator-behind-the-narrator declares, in one of the novel's numerous bracketed intrusions, "[Someone was]" (27).

The particular model of male literary ambition Groff has in her sights gets articulated by a fierce drama critic named Phoebe Delmar, who dutifully thrashes each and every one of Lotto's plays. When Mathilde finally meets her, not long before Lotto's death, Phoebe explains that the only reason she is so hard on Lotto is because she takes him seriously. "I want him to be better than he is" (342). What prevents him from meeting full artistic potential is a "sickness" she calls "Great American Artistitis," which she describes as follows:

> Ever bigger. Ever louder. Jostling for the highest perch in the hegemony. You don't think that's some sort of sickness that befalls men when they try to do art in this country? Tell me, why did Lotto write a war play? Because works about war always trump works about emotions, even if the smaller, more domestic plays are better written, smarter, more interesting. The war stories are the ones that get all the prizes. But your husband's voice is strongest when he speaks most quietly and clearly. (342)

On one level, the passage advocates for the novel that contains it. *Fates and Furies* is first and foremost a domestic drama, or a novel about marriage, the "traditional" subject for women writers going back to Austen and before. And, as Phoebe argues in a sly paraphrase of Virginia Woolf, such novels, which are often "better written, smarter, [and] more interesting" than war novels, have been traditionally devalued, not just because war trumps emotion but also because, in the literary marketplace, male authorship trumps female authorship. In Woolf's sardonic formulation, "This is an important book, the critic assumes, because it is deals with war. This is an insignificant book because it deals with the feelings of women in the drawing-room" (*A Room of One's Own* 128). Groff's novel flips this dialectic. Although she is keenly conscious throughout that she is authoring a work about marriage, this self-consciousness springboards her ongoing subversion of that very same domestic-drama tradition. And the subversion includes her portrait of male authorship, as embodied by Lancelot.

In many respects, "Great American Artistitis" is the same "sickness" that Hungerford detects not only in what she views as Wallace's arrogance and ambition but also in the machinery of his celebrity. What's more, a version of it sits at the heart of just about any traditional novel of artistic development. Such works fall under the rubric of the *künstlerroman*, or the novel of an artist's life, a variation on the traditional *bildungsroman*, or novel of education. Lotto's story, contained entirely in the novel's first half, constitutes a mini-parody of the genre. Groff's masterstroke is to subordinate Lotto's *künstlerroman* to the more interesting and vibrant domestic drama that is *Fates and Furies'* primary genre.

In traditional works of this genre, ranging from Wordsworth's *The Prelude* to Joyce's *Portrait of the Artist as a Young Man* and F. Scott Fitzgerald's *This Side of Paradise*, the narrative proceeds through the key moments in the apprentice author's life that will shape the hero's artistic development. Each moment represents an advance toward artistic fulfillment, which the hero achieves by novel's end, at which point we understand that the hero is now ready to produce the work that will confirm (not always, but usually) his genius. Hence Stephen Dedalus's famous valediction in the concluding pages of Joyce's *Portrait*: "Welcome, O life! I go to encounter for the millionth time the reality of experience and to force in the smithy of my soul the uncreated consciousness of my race" (244). Lotto's journey toward artistic fulfillment mocks the genre at each point. Lotto does not even consider himself a playwright until much later in life. Instead, Lotto spends his twenties trying, and failing, to become a successful actor. Similarly, his artistic "breakthrough" is a fluke. The same night that he accepts his vocational failure—and considers suicide as a result—he gets ruinously drunk, opens his laptop, and writes a set of scenes that he completely forgets about the next morning. When he wakes up, hungover, to find Mathilde confronting him with an open laptop, his first thought is that "he'd left porn on his laptop and she'd seen it when she had woken up. Maybe a terrible kind of porn, the worst" (82). The scene he reads, and only dimly recalls writing, has already been thoroughly revised and polished by Mathilde, as will be the case with most of his work. In a clever turn of phrase, Mathilde insists, "All along . . . hiding here in plain sight. Your true talent," to which Lotto responds, "My true talent . . . [w]as hiding" (83). Nevertheless, solely on the strength of Mathilde's insistence that he's a "genius," which Lotto confesses he "had long known . . . in his bones," he decides, "All right, then. He could be a playwright" (84).

Groff continues to subvert the genre by eliminating all subsequent struggles. Lotto does not have to prove himself to indifferent producers or directors, for Mathilde, working behind the scenes, secures funding for his first play by blackmailing her own uncle. Nor does Groff dramatize Lotto's laborious writing process. Each play appears, one after the other, as a finished product; all we see of the plays are brief excerpts, usually consisting of fictionalized depictions of events from Lotto's past that Groff has already dramatized to better effect. As for the writing itself, we later learn that "for a number of his plays, at least half, [Mathilde] would silently steal in at night and refine what he had written," with Groff's intrusive behind-the-scenes narrator adding, "[Not rewrite; edit, burnish, make glow]" (245). Lotto only dimly acknowledges all of Mathilde's backstage management. At one of his lowest moments, he wonders, "How could he live without her? . . . How would he write without her?" whereupon Groff's narrator observes, "[The buried awareness of how completely her hands reached into his work; don't look, Lotto. It'd be like looking at the sun]" (172). At every turn, Groff undercuts the Joycean model of the solitary artistic genius. Rather, she casts Lotto's artistic rise as a product of unacknowledged male privilege. As a doomed collaborator observes, "It's clear in your work. Privilege is what lets you take risks . . . Coddled. Like the

AGAINST WALLACE   137

precious egg you are" (125). And the male privilege that allows him to create is inseparable from the privilege he enjoys (but does not acknowledge) as the coddled husband of a wife who not only shapes and cocreates his work but also manages every other aspect of his life.

Wallace is far from the sole, or even the primary, target of Groff's critique. Rather, Wallace represents only a fraction of the dense network of coded references to the male literary tradition of modernist and postmodernist achievement that begins with Joyce and continues through Nabokov, Barth, and Pynchon. But as Wallace is the focus of this study, his presence will be addressed first. The two most overt links to Wallace appear near the end of the Lancelot-focused "Fates" section, and both involve Wallace's use of ellipses to signal silence in the context of a stretch of dialogue. Wallace first introduced the technique in *The Broom of the System* and carried it forward into *Infinite Jest*. The ellipses appear in stretches of dialogue in which Wallace, in homage to the work of William Gaddis, eliminates dialogue tags or scenic descriptions.[2] Groff employs the technique first in an excerpt from one of Lancelot's plays, *Ice in the Bones*, which draws upon Lotto's lonely years in a prestigious prep school. Significantly, the Dean probes "Ollie," the Lancelot figure, if he is depressed:

> DEAN: [*Opens his drawer. Under a spill of papers is something that Ollie sees, and he sits up as if goosed. The dean shuts the drawer, lifting out a rubber band, tenting it back with his thumb. He aims it Ollie's nose and lets fly. Ollie blinks. The dean sits back in his chair.*]
> DEAN: An undepressed person would have avoided that.
> OLLIE: Probably.
> DEAN: You, my friend, are a whiner.
> OLLIE: . . .
> DEAN: Ha! You look like Rudolph the Red-Nosed La-di-da.
> OLLIE: . . .
> DEAN: Ha! (177)

---

[2]For examples, see *Broom of the System*, pages 22–27, or *Infinite Jest*, pages 39–42, though the technique appears throughout both novels such that it has become one of Wallace's most prominent stylistic tics.

The excerpt itself calls to mind numerous scenes from *Infinite Jest* set in the novel's own elite prep school, Enfield Tennis Academy, particularly the "Professional Conversationalist" scene between the novel's hero, Hal Incandenza, and his father. Groff employs the technique a second time during a fight scene involving Lotto and Mathilde, with Mathilde's key lines replaced by Wallace-esque ellipses, her silence thus marking a secondary reference to Wallace's "Brief Interviews with Hideous Men" cycle, wherein a female interviewer's questions are replaced by a simple "Q.":

> "Oh my god. We are discussing the fact you wrote me into a murderer, out of nowhere, here we are again with the kid nonsense."
>
> "Nonsense?"
>
> " . . . "
>
> "Mathilde? Why are you breathing like that?"
>
> " . . . "
>
> "Mathilde? Where are you going?" (183)

In this instance, Lotto, who is trying to justify basing a murderer in one of his plays upon Mathilde, gets transformed by implication into a "hideous man," one who cannot pass up an opportunity, even in the context of a fight in which he is in the wrong, to needle his wife about giving him a child.

These two overt references to Wallace's work invite readers to interpret additional key details in the novel as also coded to invoke Wallace. For instance, the repeated references to Lotto's "glow" and its connection to his "genius" suggest a connection to *Infinite Jest*'s Hal Incandenza, the lexical and tennis prodigy who represents the closest thing in Wallace's work to a fictionalized autobiographical double, and whose last name suggests "incandescence." Like Eugenides' Leonard Bankhead and Franzen's Richard Katz, Lotto is also a tireless womanizer, possessed of a mysterious sexual charisma that somehow overcomes various physical oddities. As Danica, a college friend, observes, "If he were actually good looking he'd never be as deadly, but five minutes in a room with him, all you want to do is get naked" (42). In this respect, he lives up to his Arthurian name, as the chivalric Lancelot, eventually done in by his affair with Guinivere, was also known as Arthur's most accomplished swordsman.[3]

But perhaps the most significant link back to Wallace, and more specifically *Infinite Jest*, resides in the novel's sustained intertextual dialogue with the work of Shakespeare, perhaps an unsurprising feature in a novel about a playwright. Although Groff references nearly a half a dozen plays, including *Measure for Measure* (53), *The Comedy of Errors* (192), *Coriolanus* (312, 385), and *The Tempest* (the novel features a pivotal character named Ariel, about whom more anon), the most prominent early references are to *Hamlet*. Lotto's failed career as an actor peaks during his senior in college, during which he "shined so brilliantly" in the title role (52). Mathilde first meets him backstage after his final performance: their entire marriage, and hence the novel's primary narrative, follows directly from that first encounter. *Hamlet* is even more central to *Infinite Jest*, beginning with the title, a direct quote from the famous "graveyard scene" wherein Hamlet holds up a skull and declares, "Alas, poor Yorick? I knew him, Horatio: a fellow of infinite jest, of most excellent fancy" (V.1. 169–71). Hal's father, James Incandenza, creates the lethally entertaining film that also shares the book's title, after which he commits suicide, leaving his son Hal in a state of Hamlet-like paralysis while James's widowed wife, Avril, takes up with her own half brother, Charles C. T. Tavis, a slight inversion of the *Hamlet's* Gertrude, who, following her husband's death, marries his brother, Claudius.

Yet whereas Wallace cleaves closely to the key coordinate points Shakespeare's narrative, Groff freely inverts and departs from her model. Lotto is an anti-*Hamlet*. Although given occasionally to depression and fleeting thoughts of suicide, he is for the most part optimistic, unaware of the world around him, and uxoriously attached to his own anti-Ophelia, Mathilde. Meanwhile, Antoinette never remarries following the death of her husband, Gawain, and disowns Lotto in a jealous pique when her son informs her of his rash marriage to Mathilde. In a similar vein, late in her life, Mathilde writes a play titled *Volumnia* that recasts Shakespeare's

---

[3]In another link to the Arthurian legend, Lotto loses his virginity, and unbeknownst to him also fathers a son, with a teenage friend named Gwendolyn, this novel's Guinivere.

Coriolanus from the perspective of the title character's wife (385). As with Mathilde, in her role as Lotto's fascinating puppeteer and the novel's true protagonist, Volumnia, in Mathilde's view, is "steely, controlling," and "far more interesting than Coriolanus" (312). In all these instances, Groff looks to de-emphasize Shakespeare's male characters and elevate the women, giving them new agency and centrality, all in direct defiance of the tradition, voiced by an actor friend of Lotto's named Susannah, that "women in narratives were always defined by their relations" (77). Significantly, Susannah, who scores a long-running role in a soap opera, enjoys a much more successful acting career than does Lotto, even though she is never celebrated as such. The novel's deft references to *Hamlet* specifically and to Shakespeare more generally provide Groff with rich opportunities to disclose the sexist erasures of female agency that inform both Shakespeare and Wallace.

Groff performs numerous similar inversions throughout the bravura final movement of Lotto's narrative. For the section's first half, Groff employs a rapid temporal pace, racing through the first forty years of Lancelot's life; beginning with Chapter 5, the narrative slows down to cover a crucial several months in his creative life and a significant moment of public humiliation before dramatizing his final months. As such, this section introduces a new register in the novel, suggesting that it constitutes a coherent unit within the larger narrative.

The sequence begins with a curious fall down the exit stairs of an airplane that leaves Lotto essentially paralyzed for several months. The agent of his fall is a silent, anonymous man identified by his "tomato-colored hair and face," the "lines on his forehead," and his "madras shorts" (99). When Lotto wonders "Who would do such a thing? Why? Why to him? What had he done?", Groff's behind-the-scene narrator enigmatically informs us, "[There'd be no answers. The man was gone]" (99, 100). That latter intrusion suggests that, much the same way Mathilde serves as Lotto's puppet, so, too, is Groff introducing authorial agents to advance her plot, similar to Nabokov's use of Clare Quilty and Vivian Darkbloom to foil Humbert Humbert's control of Lolita in the novel of the same name. Groff confirms her Nabokovian intentions by appearing as herself at the writing colony that Lotto attends following his convalescence. While assessing the other artists assembled for dinner on his first night at the colony, Lotto notes a novelist who is "blond, athletic, not bad despite the breeder's gut and purple bags under her eyes" (121). He goes on to note her "lovely white foreams, as if cut from polished spruce wood" and her "round belly with the silver stretch marks on it" (121). In her acknowledgments, Groff reveals that *Fates and Furies* "began its life on the page at the MacDowell Colony, with the help of the work of Anne Carson, Evan S. Connell, Jane Gardam, Thomas Mann, [and] William Shakespeare" (391). She also praises her two sons, "Becket and Heath" (391). Groff's wording here recalls the famous passage from "On a Book Entitled *Lolita*" in which Nabokov observes, "The first little throb of *Lolita* went through me in late 1939 or early in 1940, in Paris" (*Lolita* 311). Additional features of Groff's novel deepen the Nabokovian debt. Groff's bracketed narrative intrusions perhaps owe something to similar intrusions featured in Nabokov's *Ada, or Ardor*, which are usually attributed to Ada, the narrator's sister, who appears to be deftly editing Van's account.[4] Finally, Groff twice invokes Humbert Humbert's memorable two-word account of his mother's death: "(picnic, lightning)" (10). In an authorial prolepsis, Groff's narrator reveals that a college-aged friend of Lotto, Natalie, will later die from a "Ski tumble; embolism" (135). Similarly, the narrator describes the death of Mathilde's uncle, a significant character in his own right, with another pithy two-word account: "[carjacking; crowbar]" (329).

Having effectively shifted the novel into a new Nabokovian mode, Groff amplifies the novel's metafictional and parodic agenda. Lotto's experience at the ice-covered writing colony invokes Hans Castorp's extended stay at the Swiss sanatorium in *The Magic Mountain*, while his collaboration with a young composer named Leo Sens sounds a number of parodic and metafictional notes. Robin Black, who similarly feels that the novel's wordplay "evokes Nabokov," speculates that Leo Sens might serve as "the perfect doppelgänger for a narcissist [such as Lotto], complete with Lotto's own initials" (Black). If Black is correct, then Leo is a doppelgänger in the Clare Quilty mold, that is, a double for

---

[4]Nabokov clues his reader to this aspect of the narrative at the end of Chapter 1, which concludes with an enigmatic line reading "Hue or who? Awkward. Reword," followed by this parenthetical addendum: "(marginal note in Ada Veen's late hand)" (9). Subsequent bracketed intrusions represent additional "marginal notes" presumably penciled in by Ada at some later date.

the protagonist and the novelist's double agent. In yet another instance of the Sedgwick-inflected love triangle already addressed in *The Marriage Plot* and *Freedom*, Lotto and Leo develop a homoerotic affection for each other that threatens Mathilde's hold over Lotto. When Leo plays for Lotto the first piece of music for their proposed opera, Lotto, either from artistic integrity or homophobic self-preservation, rejects the music, which seems to be directed at him, as "treacle," the melody "so sweet it ached his teeth" (147). Leo responds to this rejection by committing suicide, one of two suicides in the novel directly attributable to Lotto's narcissistic indifference, an outcome Mathilde perceives as a "victory, hot and terrible" (252).

Yet although Leo is eliminated as Lotto's collaborator, he returns, beyond the grave as it were, to collaborate with Groff's Olympian narrator. The opera Leo and Lotto collaborate on, but only sketch out in the broadest terms, constitutes one of the novel's most audacious *tours de force*. The two plan a rewriting of Antigone they title *The Antigonad*, which, in Leo's assessment, will extend the original play's submerged "Misandry" (132). The title recalls John Barth's postmodern mock epics, "Menelaid" and "Anonymiad" from *Lost in the Funhouse*, and "Dunyazadiad," "Perseid," and "Bellerophoniad" from *Chimera*. Once again, however, Groff employs these male-authored source texts to reverse the male-centered gender dynamic. The title can be cleverly glossed as "The Anti-Gonad," which reading Leo freely acknowledges when he observes that he and Lotto "can always change if we find ourselves to be pro-gonad" (133). They refer to their title character as "Go," suggesting that, unlike the passively immortal Antigone, their heroine will have more agency. The shortened name might also be a play on the splitting of "woman" into its two parts, with the difference that the "wo" prefix, from "womb," has been replaced by "go."

The unfinished opera appears in the novel in the form of Lotto's outline, or more specifically "First sketch, with notes for music" (153). Yet Groff makes clear that the sketch we are reading has been expanded by both Groff's narrator and Leo Sens, who comments via bracketed intrusions that are the narrator's usual mode of readerly communication. The opera itself dramatizes the wall between the sexes, represented here as an actual wall that separates immortal, furious Go from a construction worker named

Ros, who tries but fails to dig his way toward the unseen object of his obsession. Meanwhile, as the opera moves from the mythic past to the present day, the gods who sentenced Go to a solitary immortality have been reduced to warring "hoboes," who blow up the world in a nuclear holocaust, leaving Go "alone . . . Deathless in a dead world" (161). In *Chimera*, Barth explains his approach to mythic archetypes as a reversal of the Joycean "mythic method": "Since myths themselves are among other things poetic distillations of our ordinary psychic experience and therefore point always to daily reality, to write realistic fictions which point always to mythic archetypes is in my opinion to take the wrong and of the mythopoeic stick . . . Better to address the archetypes directly" (199). Groff's technique in *The Antigonad* borrows Barth's strategy of "addressing the archetypes directly" but parts from him in the assumption that these archetypes point disinterestedly to "ordinary psychic experience." As in her reappropriations of Shakespeare, Wallace, and Nabokov, she also revises the archetypes to disclose their inherent sexism. Leo's beyond-the-grave presence in *The Antigonad*'s creation suggests that Groff all along has been setting up Lotto as an emblem for the artist as a dangerous sexist and narcissist whose creations, like the novel's other male-authored source texts, must be interrogated and rewritten to account for the same biases.

Groff completes this section of Lotto's undoing with an extended episode set at a college theater symposium. Here she exposes the deep-rooted misogyny in both Lotto and the tradition of male authorship he embodies. In addition to Lotto, the symposium, devoted to the "Future of Theater," features a "girl prodigy in her twenties, [a] Native American dynamo in his thirties, [and an] antique voice of theater whose best work was forty years deep in the last century" (162). While Lotto and his elderly male counterpart represent the male-centered tradition of twentieth-century letters, the "girl prodigy" and "Native American dynamo" bring to the discussion the voices of women and minority writers. In this environment, Lotto feels attacked as a white male and strikes back by defending the patriarchal order in which, in his view anyway, men create the art while their wives make the babies. When the young prodigy objects, "I have a wife and I am a wife. I'm not comfortable with the gender essentialism I'm hearing here" (164), Lotto lets loose with a diatribe that reads like a parody of what Mary Allen memorably defined as John Updike's "Love of Dull Bovine Beauty":

> Listen, we're all given a finite amount of creativity, just like we're given a finite amount of life, and if a woman chooses to spend hers on creating life and not imaginary life, that's a glorious choice. When a woman has a baby, she's creating so much more than just a made-up world on the page! She's creating life itself, not just a simulacrum. No matter what Shakespeare did, it's so much less than your average illiterate woman of his age who had babies ... It's a kind of bodily genius ... Women are just as good as men—better, in many ways—but the reason for the disparity in creation is because woman have turned their creative energies inward, not outward. (165)

Lotto's speech, ostensibly an encomium to women—and to his wife, who remains resolutely childless of her own accord—participates in what Allen terms "the necessary blankness" in so much male-authored fiction. Updike in particular is pertinent here, for Lotto's disingenuous conflation of childbearing with the work of males recalls Allen's observation that, throughout his work of the 1960s at least, "Updike equates childbirth for a woman with a career for a man," a point she supports by quoting a passage from Updike's 1968 suburban sexcapade, *Couples*: "the men had stopped having careers and the women had stopped having babies" (Allen 113; *Couples* 17). As she goes on to argue, "Aside from lovemaking and childbearing, there is almost nothing for Updike's women to do" (163). But Groff might also have had Updike in mind in her playful renaming of Anigone, in *The Antigonad*, as "Go." In Updike's early story, "Wife-Wooing," the narrator, while watching his wife eat a take-out hamburger and pondering her "absolute geography," wonders, "What soul took thought and knew that adding 'wo' to man would make a woman? The difference exactly. The wide w, the receptive o. Womb" (*Pigeon Feathers* 109, 110). As is typical in his work, Updike, like Lotto in this speech, even in his "praise" of women, necessarily reduces them to their sexual organs and sexual function.

Even before he is finished, his words turn to wormwood in his mouth, but the damage is already done. The audience turns against him, and Mathilde disappears from the audience. At once, Lotto realizes, "There was an enormous crack in the world" (165). To Lotto's Updikean objection, "I'm not a misogynist! I love women," the young playwright on stage with him responds, "That's what all misogynists say. You just love to pork women" (167). In the aftermath of this public flogging, Lotto, realizing he lacks money for a cab—"He never had to pay for a thing on these jaunts, and if he did, Mathilde was there with her purse" (167)—walks back home, alone, to their hotel in an extended sequence that brilliantly parodies "The Swimmer" by John Cheever, Updike's suburban-dwelling compatriot. Like Ned Merrill, Cheever's suburban Odysseus, Lotto encounters a series of deepening humiliations on his nightmarish journey home, each one peeling away his defenses until he is left stripped down to his essential core self, which, in another nod to Updike, is that of a beloved coddled son of a controlling, imperious mother, whom he phones for succor.

During their brief collect phone call, Antoinette seizes at the thought that Mathilde has finally left him, thereby returning him, Oedipally, to his first and foremost love, herself: "I knew she'd end up hurting you. Just come home . . . and your women will take care of you" (169). The passage recalls another Updike story from the same period as "Wife-Wooing," "Flight," in which the frightful mother figure competes with the high school girlfriend of the story's hero, Allen Doe, whom the mother has already assured is a genius who will leave their small town and "fly" (50). The girlfriend, in the mother's assessment, is unworthy of her son's genius, much as Antoinette dismisses Mathilde as unworthy of Lotto. Similarly, in Updike's story, Allen, like Lotto, gets booed while performing on stage—Allen is on the high school debate team—and his subsequent humiliation incites his internal conflict between the object of his sexual passion and his mother.

The two strains—that of Updike and Cheever—reach their apogee at the section's end. In Cheever's story, Ned Merrill arrives home from his journey through his neighbor's pools only to realize that his house empty. "The doors were locked," he notes, "and the rust came off the handles onto his hands," suggesting that the house has been empty a long time, and that Ned has been delusional all along about the state of his life: rather than the exuberant suburban conqueror he imagines himself to be at the story's beginning, he is revealed at the end, through Cheever's surreal sleight of hand, to be a failure, perhaps an out-of-work divorcee, and certainly a drunk (612). Lotto, too, arrives back at the hotel defeated, his feet bleeding, his face sunburnt, his mouth dry (Groff 173). In a deft reversal of Cheever's story, however, Mathilde is not only waiting for him, but "naked under the sheet" and smilingly receptive (173). Her receptivity is as surreal and dreamlike as Cheever's dark unmasking, and in fact should be read as a deliberate parody of the male tradition that Updike and Cheever both represent. Updike's Allen, following his public embarrassment at the debate, finds solace in his girlfriend's embrace: "For the first time, on that ride home, I felt what it was to bury a humiliation in the body of a woman" (63). Groff's Mathilde provides that same solace but in such an overt way that her response discloses how female characters in Updike and his contemporaries are "always defined by their relations" (Groff 77). As Mathilde feeds him water and salmon and chocolate cake, she slyly tells him, "You win. No matter what, you win. It all works out for you in the end. Always. Someone or something's looking out for you. It's maddening" (175). One of the people looking out for him is Groff's Olympian narrator, who has staged this metafictional episode, and Mathilde's male-fantasy response, as a critique of the work of those writers lurking in the episode's intertextual background.

As already pointed out, Lotto's *kunstleroman* occupies the novel's first half; the second half narrates Mathilde's life in a strategy that parallels Mathilde's own decision to rewrite *Corialanus* as Volumnia's story. Like Volumnia, Mathilde, as Lotto's returning son Roland observes, is "the untold story," "the mystery," and "the interesting one" (272). Mathilde's section, titled "Furies," does more than fill out the details of their marriage: rather, as Black observes, it presents an entirely different set of events. Unfortunately, a full discussion of that remarkable unfolding of events lies outside the scope of this essay, which focuses on Groff's scalpel-sharp dissection of the male literary tradition that includes Nabokov, Updike, Cheever, Barth, and, most pertinent to this study, Wallace.

The model of literary genius that Wallace has come to represent has been figured in literary culture as primarily male. The pushback against this model is both necessary and useful. Hungerford's unconvincing justification for ignoring Wallace in many respects reenforces the gender dichotomy that Hungerford and the other bloggers decry. The aggressive refusal to engage with a book like *Infinite Jest* casts the work, and the tradition from which it emerged, into a gendered oblivion of "lit-bros." Groff's novel, conversely, confronts that tradition on its own terms, sometimes in its own language, and incorporates it into a traditionally "female" literary tradition of domestic fiction. As such, she explodes the gendered essentialism that would assign high literary achievement to male writers and emotional, domestic drama solely to women.

Conclusion

Love and Cruelty

The books and authors selected for analysis here are not meant to be exhaustive. I chose them because they lay out the broadest contours of the Wallace Effect as it has emerged over the past decade or so. At one level, the Wallace Effect is the natural reaction to the immense, and to some, outsized stature Wallace has achieved in the contemporary US literary imagination. Literary success, particularly the level that Wallace has achieved, is bound to spark envy, and so it should not be surprising that Wallace's contemporaries have pushed back against the singularity of his position. Yet that push back is also of a piece with Wallace's own fictional project, which is openly competitive and anxious about its pedigree of artistic influences. In a way relatively unique even in the context of postmodern metafiction, Wallace's work is uniquely conspicuous in the battles it wages with its literary precursors. And so the books chosen here either fill out telling gaps in Wallace's self-proclaimed list of patriarchs for his patricide or, more importantly, use Wallace's own metafictional strategies of literary score settling to settle scores with Wallace himself.

Perhaps the most animating motif in Wallace's patricidal project is his reformulation of Barth's lovemaking model for storytelling, which I explore at length in Chapter 1. As quoted already, narrative, Barth argues, is a "love relation, not a rape; its success depend[s] upon the reader's consent and co-operation, which she [can] withhold or at any moment withdraw" (*Chimera* 28). Wallace's revision of this model, in "Westward" and in his early interviews, sits at the core of his broader critique of metafictional self-reflexivity. If Barth's work is "the act of a lonely solipsist's self-love," as Wallace insists, then his own work will more accurately reflect a "love relation" because it will "perpetrate the kind of special cruelty only real lovers can inflict" (*Girl* 332). Wallace's cruelty encompasses both his public rebukes of his literary forebears and the challenges he imposes upon his readers. The texts addressed in the Wallace Effect section of this volume don't just respond to these two aspects of Wallace's project; rather, they deploy Wallace's own techniques against him. Both the love triangles in *The Marriage Plot* and *Freedom* and the artistically fertile marriages in *The Tidewater Tales* and *Fates and Furies* interrogate and supplement Barth and Wallace's "love-relation" metaphor. Meanwhile, Eugenides' Leonard Bankhead, Messud's Bootie Tubb and Murray Thwaite, and Franzen's Richard Katz invoke Wallace in ways that are alternately affectionate and cruel. The Wallace Effect, while certainly grounded in literary envy, is also a product of love, and if true love in Wallace's world is cruel, then cruelty will be repaid in kind. "Criticism is response," J. D. Steelritter observes in "Westward." "Which is good" (240).

Franzen's Contract/Status dialectic, as spelled out in his essay "Mr. Difficult" and explored in Chapter 5, also animates much of the work resulting from the Wallace Effect. While Franzen never names Wallace directly, it is unlikely that Wallace was far from his mind when he was developing his thesis. For instance, when Franzen argues that, in the Contract model, the "deepest purpose of reading and writing fiction is to sustain a sense of connectedness, to resist existential loneliness," he channels Wallace's "explicit" belief that "fiction is a solution, the *best* solution, to existential solitude" ("Mr. Difficult" 100; *Farther* 44). Yet Franzen also explains that, for the Status writer, "Easy fiction has little value . . . Pleasure that demands hard work, the slow penetration of mystery, the outlasting of lesser readers, is the pleasure most worth having" (100). This latter formulation deftly paraphrases Wallace's description of "serious" art's necessary difficulty, which is designed to "make you uncomfortable, or to force you to work hard to access its pleasure, the same way that in real life true pleasure is the by-product of hard work and discomfort" (*Conversations* 22). Although the "Mr.

Difficult" in the essay's title refers specifically to William Gaddis, this clear allusion to Wallace broadens the title's possible referents.

Strikingly, the four novels that wrestle most directly with Wallace's reputation as the leading Status writer of his generation all do so in the context of what Franzen would deem Contract novels. "In my bones," Franzen declares, "I'm a Contract kind of person," and so his books, beginning with *The Corrections* and including *Freedom*, are Contract books, designed for readerly pleasure and, by extension, the bestseller lists. But *The Marriage Plot*, *Emperor's Children*, and *Fates and Furies* were also bestsellers, widely reviewed in the mainstream press and adopted in book clubs all across the country. In each text, the fictionalized Wallace figure is toppled from his position on Mount Status and brought back to earth, humbled and humiliated but also loved and celebrated.

The texts addressed here also share a sustained rather than glancing relationship to Wallace's project. Barth's *Tidewater Tales* represents an almost point-by-point correction of the flaws Wallace was concurrently itemizing in Barth's own fiction. Powers's *Prisoner's Dilemma* exemplifies a startling number of advances on traditional postmodern metafiction that Wallace was groping toward in his own work. Messud's *Emperor's Children* provides a pointed alternative view of literary irony that supplements Powers's Rorty-inflected embrace of same. Bankhead, Katz, and Groff's Lotto are not just walk-on allusions to Wallace but protagonists in their respective texts.

That being said, Wallace's ghostly presence can be detected in a number of other texts that I did not address in this volume but wish to touch upon here, in the hope of perhaps spurring additional scholarship in this vein. Although Richard Powers was obviously not thinking of Wallace while writing *Prisoner's Dilemma*, he might have been doing so in his 2009 "enhancement" *Generosity*, which features an aspiring creative nonfiction writer named Russell Stone who meets a woman possibly endowed with a genetic propensity for happiness. Wallace also lurks in the background of *Purity* (2015), Franzen's follow-up to *Freedom*. The storyline involving the Julian Assange-like Internet activist Andreas Wolf plays out against an elaborate *Hamlet* motif that inevitably calls to mind *Infinite Jest*. What's more, Wolf ends his narrative by taking his own life. Jonathan Lethem's *Chronic City* (2009), a surreal encomium to marijuana, features a fictional "gigantic novel entitled *Obstinate

Dust" by a one Ralph Warden Meeker that the narrator keeps encountering over and over again on the subways and streets of Brooklyn (43). And Jennifer Egan's novel in stories, *A Visit from the Goon Squad* (2010), includes a Wallace-esque journalist whose work includes footnotes intended to "inject[] a whiff of cracked leather bindings into pop-cultural observation" (168). While these Wallace references seem on the surface to be merely playful, they might prove on closer inspection to constitute a more complex entanglement with Wallace's work along the lines of the readings provided in this volume.

Finally, what I have been calling Wallace's "ghostly presence" in these novels draws its inspiration from the figure of James Incandenza's wraith, who, near the end of *Infinite Jest*, appears to Don Gately and explains that he can "never speak right to anybody . . . and [has] to use somebody's like internal brain-voice if he wanted to communicate something" (831). Incandenza's means of communication affirms one of Wallace's most famous convictions about the purpose of fiction, namely that it "is an act of communication between one human being and another" (*Supposedly* 144). A radical filmmaker referred to throughout the novel as the *auteur*, Incandenza invokes the figure of the author, whose ghostly presence manifests in the act of reading. For many readers, Wallace's work, and *Infinite Jest* in particular, constitutes a uniquely intimate relationship between writer and reader. As mentioned in the introduction, Lipsky invokes something of this quality when he credits Wallace with capturing "everybody's brain voice" (xxviii). Those novelists who felt compelled to bring some revenant of Wallace into their fiction are merely taking a cue from the man himself. For it is no accident that the second paragraph of *Infinite Jest*, encountered at the very beginning of the reader's long, arduous, and transformative push through the text, consists of a single, comforting sentence: "I am in here" (3).

ACKNOWLEDGMENTS

I first wish to thank Stephen J. Burn, series editor, esteemed colleague, and cherished friend. Stephen's immediate and ongoing enthusiasm for this project spurred me to its completion. He also carefully read through the manuscript and pointed me in the direction of several key sources I had overlooked. The late Charles Harris solicited and carefully edited an earlier and considerably more attenuated version of the Barth essay included here, and which originally appeared in *John Barth: A Body of Words*, which Charles edited with Gabrielle Dean. Thanks also to Beatrice Pire, who invited me to be the keynote speaker at the "Infinite Wallace Paris International Conference" in September 2014, where I delivered an early draft of "The Rival Lover" essay on Wallace and Eugenides' *The Marriage Plot*, a version of which first appeared in *Modern Fiction Studies*. It has been a pleasure and an honor to work once again with Haaris Naqvi and Mary Al-Sayed and the whole team at Bloomsbury. I wish to extend a wide-ranging thank-you to the growing community of Wallace scholars whose work and companionship have meant so much to me over the last decade or so, a list that includes Mary Holland, Ralph Clare, Toon Staes, Allard den Dulk, Andrew Warren, Brad Fest, Philip Sayers, David Letzler, Conley Routers, Patrick O'Donnell, Kasia Boddy, Paul Quinn, Roberto Natalini, Clare Hayes-Brady, David Evans, Brian McHale, Andrew Hoberek, Tony McMahon, Daniela Franca Joffe, and Jamie Redgate. I am indebted to Rhodes College for awarding me a Faculty Development Endowment grant in the summer of 2014 to aid me in drafting two essays in this volume. The remarkably committed Rhodes students from my three Senior Seminars on Wallace's *Infinite Jest* were invaluable in shaping, sharpening, and deepening my understanding of several of the works addressed here. I am grateful to all my colleagues in the Rhodes College English Department, who have provided me with a model of collegiality and scholarly rigor that has guided my professional life for more than twenty years. A special thanks to Leslie Petty and Gordon Bigelow for unflagging support throughout the writing of this book, and to Lorie Yearwood for helping me compile the bibliography. Finally, thanks to my boys, Graham, Evan, and Julian, for keeping me grounded, and to my amazing spouse, Rebecca Finlayson, to whom this book, completed on the eve of our twentieth wedding anniversary, is dedicated.

BIBLIOGRAPHY

Allen, Mary. "John Updike's Love of 'Dull Bovine Beauty.'" *The Necessary Blankness: Women in Major American Fiction of the Nineteen Sixties.* Urbana: University of Illinois Press, 1976. 97–132.

Allen, Mary. *The Necessary Blankness.* Chicago: University of Illinois Press, 1976.

Amis, Martin. "The Voice of the Lonely Crowd." *The Guardian.com.* June 1, 2002. Web. https://www.theguardian.com/books /2002/jun/01/ philosophy.society. Accessed April 10, 2017.

Auden, W.H. *Selected Poems: New Edition.* Ed. Edward Mendelson. New York: Vintage Books, 1979.

Barth, John. *Chimera.* New York: Random House, 1972.

Barth, John. *The End of the Road.* New York: Appleton Century Crofts, 1958; rev. ed., Garden City, NY: Doubleday, 1967.

Barth, John. *The Floating Opera.* New York: Appleton Century Crofts, 1956; rev. ed., Garden City, NY: Doubleday, 1967.

Barth, John. *The Friday Book.* New York: Putnam, 1984.

Barth, John. *Further Fridays: Essays, Lectures, and Other Nonfiction, 1984–1994.* Boston: Little, Brown, 1995.

Barth, John. *Giles Goat-Boy; or, The Revised New Syllabus.* Garden City, NY: Doubleday, 1966.

Barth, John. *LETTERS.* New York: Putnam, 1979.

Barth, John. "The Literature of Exhaustion." *The Friday Book: Essays and Other Nonfiction.* New York: Putnam, 1984.

Barth, John. *Lost in the Funhouse: Fiction for Print, Tape, Live Voice.* New York: Doubleday, 1968.

Barth, John. *On with the Story: A Floating Opera.* Boston: Little, Brown, 1994.

Barth, John. *Sabbatical: A Romance.* New York: Putnam, 1982.

Barth, John. *The Sot-Weed Factor.* Garden City, NY: Doubleday, 1960.

Barth, John. *The Tidewater Tales: A Novel.* New York: Putnam, 1987.

Barthes, Roland. *A Lover's Discourse: Fragments.* Trans. Richard Howard. New York: Hill and Wang, 1978.

Beers, David. "Irony Is Dead! Long Live Irony." *Salon.com*. September 9, 2001. Web. http://www.salon.com/2001/09/25/irony_lives/. Accessed April 10, 2017.

Bergström, Catherine Walker. "Recognizing the Ache of the Other: Jonathan Franzen's Reasons for Bothering." *Ethics and Poetics: Ethical Recognitions and Social Reconfigurations in Modern Narratives*. Ed. Margrét Gunnarsdôttir Champion and Irina Rasmussen Goloubeva. Newcastle: Cambridge Scholars, 2014. 107–34.

Bernhard, Thomas. *Correction*. Trans. Sophie Wilkins. New York: Alfred A. Knopf, 1979.

Bernhard, Thomas. *Wittgenstein's Nephew: A Friendship*. Trans. David McLintock. New York: Alfred A. Knopf, 1988.

Black, Robin. "Lauren Groff's *Fates and Furies*." *New York Times Book Review*, September 8, 2015. 1.

Bloom, Harold. *The Anxiety of Influence: A Theory of Poetry*. New York: Oxford University Press, 1973.

Boswell, Marshall, ed. *David Foster Wallace and "The Long Thing."* New York: Bloomsbury, 2014.

Boswell, Marshall. "Trickle-Down Citizenship: Taxes and Civic Responsibility in *The Pale King*." *David Foster Wallace and "The Long Thing."* Ed. Marshall Boswell. New York: Bloomsbury, 2014. 209–25.

Boswell, Marshall. *Understanding David Foster Wallace*. Columbia: University of South Carolina Press, 2003.

Boswell, Marshall, and Stephen J. Burn, eds. *A Companion to David Foster Wallace Studies*. New York: Palgrave MacMillan, 2013.

Bresnan, Mark. "'Consistently Original Perennially Unheard Of': Punk, Margin, and the Mainstream in Jonathan Franzen's *Freedom*." *Write in Tune: Contemporary Music in Fiction*. Ed. Erich Hertz and Jeffrey Roessner. New York: Bloomsbury, 2014. 31–42.

Bruni, Frank. "The Grunge American Novel." *New York Times Magazine*. March 24, 1996. 38–41.

Burn, Stephen J. *Jonathan Franzen at the End of Postmodernism*. London: Continuum International, 2008.

Burn, Stephen J., and Peter Dempsey, eds. *Intersections: Essays on Richard Powers*. Champaign, IL: Dalkey Archive Press, 2006.

Butler, Nickolas. *Shotgun Lovesongs*. New York: Thomas Dunne Books, 2014.

Carmichael, Thomas. "Postmodernism Reconsidered: The Return of the Real in John Barth's *Sabbatical* and *The Tidewater Tales*." *Revue francaise d'etudes americaines* 62, no. 1 (1994): 329–38.

Cheever, John. *The Stories of John Cheever*. New York: Alfred A. Knopf, 1978.

Clark, Jonathan Russell. "Reclaiming David Foster Wallace from the
   Lit-Bros." Literary Hub.com. August 20, 2015.http://lithub.com/
   reclaiming-david-foster-wallace-from-the-lit-bros/. Accessed August
   11, 2017.
Clavier, Berndt. *John Barth and Postmodernism: Spatiality, Travel,
   Montage.* New York: Peter Lang, 2008.
Coover, Robert. *The Public Burning.* New York: Viking Press, 1977.
Dempsey, Peter. "Face the Music." *The Guardian.com.* March 29,
   2003. Web. https://www.theguardian.com/books/2003/mar/29/
   featuresreviews.guardianreview13. Accessed March 30, 2018.
den Dulk, Allard. "Boredom, Irony, and Anxiety: Wallace and the
   Kierkegaardian View of the Self." *David Foster Wallace and "The
   Long Thing."* Ed. Marshall Boswell. New York: Bloomsbury,
   2014. 43–60.
Dewey, Joseph. *Understanding Richard Powers.* Columbia: University of
   South Carolina Press, 2002.
Dierdre, Coyle. "Men Recommend David Foster Wallace to Me." Electric
   Literature.com. April 17, 2016. https://electricliterature.com/men-
   recommend-david-foster-wallace-to-me-7889a9dc6f03. Accessed
   August 11, 2017.
Dodero, Camille. "Gen (X + Y) + WTC =?" *Alternet.org.* September
   20, 2001. Web. http://www.alternet.org/story/ 11562/gen_%28x_
   %2B_y%29_%2B_wtc_%3D_. Accessed April 10, 2017.
Egan, Jennifer. *A Visit from the Goon Squad.* New York: Alfred
   A. Knopf, 2010.
Evans, David H. "'The Chains of Not Choosing': Free Will and Faith in
   William James and David Foster Wallace." *A Companion to David
   Foster Wallace Studies.* Ed. Marshall Boswell and Stephen Burn.
   New York: Palgrave MacMillan, 2013. 171–90.
Eugenides, Jeffrey. "Interview." *A "Marriage Plot" Full of Intellectual
   Angst.* By Terry Gross. *Fresh Air.* National Public Radio, New York.
   October 11, 2011. Web. http://www.npr.org/2011/10/11/140949453/a-
   marriage-plot-full-of-intellectual-angst. Accessed July 30, 2018.
Eugenides, Jeffrey. "Interview." *Questions for Jeffrey Eugenides.* By Jessica
   Grose. *Slate.com.* October 10, 2011. Web. http://www.slate.com/
   articles/arts/interrogation/2011/10/jeffrey_eugenides_interview_the_
   marriage_plot_and_david_foster_w.html. Accessed July 30, 2018.
Eugenides, Jeffrey. *The Marriage Plot.* New York: Farrar, Straus and
   Giroux, 2011.
Fischer, Molly. "Why Literary Chauvinists Love David Foster Wallace."
   TheCut.com. August 12, 2015. https://www.thecut.com/2015/08/
   david-foster-wallace-beloved-author-of-bros.html. Accessed August
   11, 2017.

Fogel, Stan, and Gordon Slethaug. *Understanding John Barth*. Columbia: University of South Carolina Press, 1990.

Franzen, Jonathan. *The Discomfort Zone: A Personal History*. New York: Farrar, Straus and Giroux, 2006.

Franzen, Jonathan. *Farther Away: Essays*. New York: Farrar, Straus and Giroux, 2012.

Franzen, Jonathan. *Freedom*. New York: Farrar, Straus and Giroux, 2010.

Franzen, Jonathan. "Jonathan Franzen on the Book, the Backlash, His Background." NPR.com. September 9, 2010. Web. http://www.npr.org/2010/09/09/129747555/franzen-on-the-book-the-backlash-his-background. Accessed May 23, 2017.

Franzen, Jonathan. "Jonathan Franzen on the Naming of Richard Katz in *Freedom*." Oprah.com. Web. http://www.oprah.com/oprahsbookclub/jonathan-franzen-on-naming-richard-katz-in-freedom-video. Accessed May 23, 2017.

Franzen, Jonathan. "Modern Life Has Become Too Distracting." *TheGuardian.com*. October 2, 2011. Web. https://www.theguardian.com/books/2015/oct/02/jonathan-franzen-writing-freedom. Accessed May 23, 2017.

Franzen, Jonathan. "Mr. Difficult." *New Yorker*, September 30, 2002. 100–11.

Franzen, Jonathan. *Purity*. New York: Farrar, Straus and Giroux, 2015.

Franzen, Jonathan. *Strong Motion*. New York: Farrar, Straus and Giroux, 1992.

Gass, William. *Habitations of the Word: Essays*. New York: Simon & Schuster, 1985.

Gass, William. *Omensetter's Luck*. New York: New American Library, 1966.

Gilbert, Sandra M., and Susan Gubar. *The Madwoman in the Attic: The Woman Writer and the Nineteenth-Century Literary Imagination*. New Haven, CT: Yale University Press, 1979.

Goethe, Johann Wolfgang von. *The Sorrows of Young Werther and Novella*. Trans. Elizabeth Mayer and Louise Brogan. Poems trans. W. H. Auden. New York: Vintage, 1971.

Groff, Lauren. *Fates and Furies*. New York: Riverhead Books, 2015.

Groff, Lauren. "Interview." Otherppl.com. OTHERPPL with Brad LIsti: Episode 51—Lauren Groff. March 11, 2012. http://otherppl.com/lauren-groff-interview/. Accessed August 11, 2017.

Handke, Peter. *A Sorrow beyond Dreams*. Trans. Ralph Manheim. Introduction by Jeffrey Eugenides. New York: New York Review Books, 2002.

Harris, Charles. "The Anxiety of Influence: The John Barth/David Foster Wallace Connection." *Critique: Studies in Contemporary Fiction 55*, no. 2 (2014): 103–26.

Harris, Charles. *Passionate Virtuosity: The Fiction of John Barth.* Urbana: University of Illinois Press, 1983.

Hayes-Brady, Clare. "'. . .': Language, Gender, and Modes of Power in the Work of David Foster Wallace." *A Companion to David Foster Wallace Studies.* Ed. Marshall Boswell and Stephen Burn. New York: Palgrave MacMillan, 2013. 131–50.

Hermanson, Scott. "Just Behind the Billboard: The Instability of Prisoner's Dilemma." *Intersections: Essays on Richard Powers.* Ed. Stephen J. Burn and Peter Dempsey. Champaign, IL: Dalkey Archive Press, 2008. 60–74.

Hoberek, Andrew. "The Novel after David Foster Wallace." *A Companion to David Foster Wallace Studies.* Ed. Marshall Boswell and Stephen Burn. New York: Palgrave MacMillan, 2013. 211–39.

Hungerford, Amy. "On Not Reading." TheChronicle.com. Chronicle Review. September 11, 2016. http://www.chronicle.com/article/On-Refusing-to-Read/237717. Accessed August 11, 2017.

Jackson, McNally. "The DFW-Eugenides Plot." *McNally Jackson Bookmongers. Tumblr.com.* July 21, 2011. Web. http://mcnallyjackson.tumblr.com/post/7891911198/the-dfw-eugenides-plot. Accessed July 30, 2018.

James, Henry. "The Art of Fiction." *The Tales of Henry James.* Ed. Christof Wegelin. New York: W. W. Norton, 1983. 345–62.

James, Henry. "Preface." *Portrait of a Lady. The New York Edition of Henry James* Vol. 3. New York: Charles Scribner's Sons, 1908. V–xxi.

James, William. "The Moral Equivalent of War." *The Writings of William James.* Ed. John J. McDermott. Chicago, IL: University of Chicago Press, 1977. 660–71.

James, William. *The Varieties of Religious Experience: A Study in Human Nature.* Cambridge: The Riverside Press, 1902.

Jarvis, Lee. "Spotlight Essay/News and Information: Newspaper Headlines." *September 11 in Popular Culture: A Guide.* Ed. Sara E. Quay and Amy M. Damico. Santa Barbara, CA: Greenwood, 2010. 76–77.

Jenner, Paul. "Jonathan Franzen's *Freedom* and 'the Great National Tragedy.'" *9/11: Topics in Contemporary North American Literature.* Ed. Catherine Morley. London: Bloomsbury, 2016. 167–84.

Johnson, Samuel. *Johnson: Prose and Poetry.* Selected Mona Wilson. Cambridge, MA: Harvard University Press, 1967.

Joyce, James. *A Portrait of the Artist as a Young Man.* Ed. Hans Gabler with Walter Hettche. New York: Vintage International, 1993.

Kakutani, Michiko. "Life in Cleveland, 1990." *New York Times*,
    December 27, 1986. 14.

Keeble, Arin. "Marriage, Relationships, and 9/11: The Seismographic
    Narratives of *Falling Man, The Good Life,* and *The Emperor's
    Children.*" *Modern Language Review* 106, no. 2 (2011): 355–73.

Kelly, Adam. "David Foster Wallace and the Novel of Ideas." *David
    Foster Wallace and "The Long Thing."* Ed. Marshall Boswell.
    New York: Bloomsbury, 2014. 3–22.

Kirn, Walter. "Long Hot Novel." *New York Observer*, February 6,
    1996. 54–55.

Kundera, Milan. *The Art of the Novel.* Trans. Linda Asher. New York:
    Grove Press, 1986.

Kundera, Milan. *Testaments Betrayed: An Essay in Nine Parts.* Trans.
    Linda Asher. New York: HarperCollins, 1995.

LeClair, Tom. "The Prodigious Fiction of Richard Powers, William
    Vollmann, and David Foster Wallace." *Critique: Studies in
    Contemporary Fiction* 38, no. 1 (1996): 12–37.

Lethem, Jonathan. *Chronic City.* New York: Doubleday, 2009.

Lipiksy, David. *Although of Course You End Up Becoming Yourself: A
    Road Trip with David Foster Wallace.* New York: Broadway, 2010.

Luft, David S. *Robert Musil and the Crisis of European Culture 1880–
    1942.* Los Angeles: University of California Press, 1980.

Mahon, Áine. "Achieving Their Country: Richard Rorty and Jonathan
    Franzen." *Philosophy and Literature* 38, no. 1 (April 2014): 90–109.

Marcus, Ben. "Why Experimental Fiction Threatens To Destroy
    Publishing, Jonathan Franzen, and Life as We Know It: A Correction."
    Harper's Magazine, October 2005. 39–52 (Folio).

Mason, Wyatt. "You Don't Like It? You Don't Have to Play." *London
    Review of Books* 26, no. 22 (2004): 17–19.

Max, D. T. *Every Love Story Is a Ghost Story: A Life of David Foster
    Wallace.* New York: Penguin, 2012.

McGarry, Jessye "Why I'm Waiting for the Right Man to Tell Me I Should
    Read 'Infinite Jest.'" Reductress.com. Thoughts, January 24, 2017.
    http://reductress.com/post/why-im-waiting-for-the-right-man-to-tell-
    me-to-read-infinite-jest/. Accessed August 11, 2017.

Messud, Claire. *The Emperor's Children.* New York: Alfred
    A. Knopf, 2006.

Moore, Steven Moore. *The Novel: An Alternative History, 1600–1800.*
    New York: Bloomsbury, 2013.

Nabokov, Vladimir. *Ada, or Ardor.* New York. McGraw-Hill, 1969.

Nabokov, Vladimir. *Lolita.* New York: G. P. Putnam & Sons, 1955.

Nabokov, Vladimir. *Speak, Memory.* New York: Random House, 1966.

Oates, Nathan. "Political Stories: The Individual in Contemporary Fiction." *The Missouri Review* 30, no. 3 (2007): 156–71.

O'Roarke, Meghan. "The End of Irony." *New York Times*, August 27, 2006. 71.

Perry, Grace, "5 Footnotes from *Infinite Jest* That'll Get Him Rock Hard." Reductress.com. Issue 24.1—Love and Sex, March 4, 2016. http://reductress.com/post/5-footnotes-from-infinite-jest-thatll-get-his-dick-rock-hard/. Accessed August 11, 2017.

Powers, Richard. "The Art of Fiction CLXXV. Interview by Kevin Berger." *The Paris Review* 44, no. 164 (2003): 107–38.

Powers, Richard. *Generosity: An Enhancement.* New York: Farrar, Straus and Giroux, 2009.

Powers, Richard. *Prisoner's Dilemma.* New York: Beech Tree, 1988.

Rorty, Richard. *Contingency, Irony, and Solidarity.* Cambridge: Cambridge University Press, 1989.

Roth, Philip. *The Counterlife.* New York: Farrar, Straus and Giroux, 1986.

Roth, Philip. *The Plot against America.* New York: Houghton Mifflin, 2004.

Said, Edward. *Beginnings: Intention and Method.* New York: Basic, 1975.

Savu, Laura. "A Difficult Dialectic: Reading the Discourses of Love in Jeffrey Eugenides's *The Marriage Plot.*" *Americana: E-Journal of American Studies in Hungary* 8, no. 2 (2012). Web. http://americanaejournal.hu/vol8no2/savu. Accessed July 30, 2018.

Scott, A. O. "The Panic of Influence." *New York Review of Books* 47, no. 2 (2000): 39–43.

Sedgwick, Eve Kosofsky. *Between Men: English Literature and Male Homosocial Desire.* New York: Columbia University Press, 1985.

Simpson, David. "'Telling it Like It Isn't." *Literature after 9/11.* Ed., Ann Kenniston and Jeanne Follansbee Quinn, London: Routledge, 2008. 209–23.

Thomas Tracey. "The Formative Years: David Foster Wallace's Philsophical Influences and *The Broom of the System.*" *Gesturing Toward Reality: David Foster Wallace and Philosophy.* Ed. Robert K. Bolger and Scott Korb. New York: Bloomsbury, 2014.

Updike, John. *Couples.* New York: Alfred A. Knopf, 1968.

Updike, John. *Pigeon Feathers.* New York: Alfred A. Knopf, 1962.

Wallace, David Foster. *Both Flesh and Not.* New York: Little, Brown, 2012.

Wallace, David Foster. *Brief Interviews with Hideous Men.* New York. Little, Brown, 1999.

Wallace, David Foster. *The Broom of the System.* New York: Penguin, 1987.

Wallace, David Foster. *Consider the Lobster and Other Essays.*
New York: Little, Brown, 2005.

Wallace, David Foster. *Conversations with David Foster Wallace.* Ed.
Stephen Burn. Jackson: University Press of Mississippi, 2012.

Wallace, David Foster. *Fate, Time, and Language: An Essay on Free
Will.* Ed. Steven M. Cahn and Maureen Eckert. New York: Columbia
University Press, 2011.

Wallace, David Foster. *Girl with Curious Hair.* New York: W. W. Norton,
1989.

Wallace, David Foster. *Infinite Jest.* New York: Little, Brown, 1996.

Wallace, David Foster. "Interview." *The Charlie Rose Show.* March 27,
1997. Web. https://www.youtube.com/watch?v=vAT9V2wHx3M.
Accessed May 23, 2017.

Wallace, David Foster. "A Lost 1996 Interview With David Foster
Wallace." Interview by Christopher Lydon. Reprinted on *Medium.
com.* December 21, 2014. Web. https://medium.com/@kunaljasty/a-
lost-1996-interview-with-david-foster-wallace-63987d93c2c. Accessed
March 28, 2017.

Wallace, David Foster. *Oblivion.* New York: Little, Brown, 2004.

Wallace, David Foster. *Quo Vadis—Introduction. Review of
Contemporary Fiction* 16, no. 1 (1999): 7–8.

Wallace, David Foster. *A Supposedly Fun Thing I'll Never Do Again.*
New York: Little, Brown, 1997.

Wallace, David Foster. *This Is Water. Some Thoughts, Delivered
on a Significant Occasion, about Living a Compassionate Life.*
New York: Little, Brown, 2009.

Wilson, Kristian. "This Woman Has Been Eating *Infinite Jest* Page-by-
Page for over a Year." Bustle.com. July 11, 2017. https://www.bustle.
com/p/this-woman-has-been-eating-infinite-jest-page-by-page-for-over-
a-year-64505?utm_term=share. Accessed August 11, 2017.

Wittgenstein, Ludwig. *The Philosophical Investigations.* Trans. G. E. M.
Anscombe. New York: Macmillan, 1953.

Wood, James. "Brain Drain." *New Yorker,* October 5, 2009. 80–83.

Wood, James. "The Digressionist." *New Republic,* August 9, 2004. 26–31.

Wood, James. *How Fiction Works.* New York: Farrar, Straus and
Giroux, 2008.

Wood, James. *The Irresponsible Self: On Laughter and the Novel.*
New York: Farrar, Straus and Giroux, 2004.

Wood, James. "Remembering David Foster Wallace." *Reluctant Habits,*
September 15, 2008. Web. http://www.edrants.com/remembering-
david-foster-wallace/. Accessed June 15, 2017.

Woolf, Virginia. *A Room of One's Own.* New York: Harcourt,
Brace, 1929.

Zeigler, Heide. *John Barth.* New York: Methuen, 1987.

INDEX

and Henry James 91
"Here and There" 20
Infinite Jest 2, 5 n.4, 6, 7, 8, 8n6,
    17, 20 n.1, 54, 61, 63, 70, 72
    n.3, 73–4, 77 n.5, 82, 83–6,
    92, 94–5, 98–9, 106, 110, 113,
    125–33, 137, 138, 139, 146,
    151, 152
interview with McCaffery 5, 7,
    70, 72 n.3, 92, 104
interview with Rose 110
and irony 6, 11, 16, 38–41, 43,
    55–6, 68, 70, 73, 82, 84, 89–
    91, 93, 98
"John Billy" 4
Kenyon College Commencement
    Speech (2005) 75, 86, 107
"Little Expressionless Animals" 6
"Lyndon" 4
and Messud 57, 83–9, 92–5, 97–
    9, 102, 151
and metafiction 4, 6, 7, 9, 15,
    17–18, 19, 37, 61, 65, 67–9,
    149–50, 151
"My Appearance" 6, 113
Oblivion 54, 91
"Octet" 113
The Pale King 74 n.4, 86, 93,
    112, 116
"Philosophy and the Mirror of
    Nature" 54
in pop culture 2, 12, 84
and postmodernism 1, 2, 4, 6, 9,
    10, 15, 16, 18, 19, 21, 37, 38–
    41, 47, 48, 61–3, 65, 67, 70,
    73, 74 n.4, 75, 84, 89–90, 92,
    93, 96, 99, 101, 137, 149, 151
and Powers 39, 101, 151
and Pynchon 2–3, 3 nn.1–2, 8–9,
    8 n.6, 15, 39, 93, 137
review of Hix's *Morte D'Author:
    An Autopsy* 4 n.3
and Rorty 54–6
and self-consciousness 6, 16, 17,
    19, 38, 63, 70, 90, 97, 103–4,
    113

"Shipping Out" ("A Supposedly
    Fun Thing I'll Never Do
    Again") 7
"The Soul is Not a Smithy" 112
*A Supposedly Fun Thing I'll Never
    Do Again* 64, 82, 110, 152
"Tennis, Trigonometry, and
    Tornadoes" ("Derivative Sport
    in Tornado Alley") 7
This Is Water 75, 107
"Ticket to the Fair" ("Getting
    Away from Already Being
    Pretty Much Away from It
    All") 7
"Westward the Course of
    Empire Takes its Way" 4, 6, 7,
    10, 11, 16–21, 20 n.2, 28, 29,
    35–6, 67–9, 150
and William James 74–5, 74 n.4,
    86, 114
and Wittgenstein 54–5, 54 n.2,
    57, 112
and Wood 87–93
Wallace, Irving
    The Seven Minutes 25
Wallace, John David 56
Wallace Effect 8, 10–11, 149–50
    definition of 1
Waugh, Evelyn 23
Wharton, Edith 89
Winfrey, Oprah 107 n.2, 121 n.5
Wittgenstein, Ludwig 54–5, 54 n.2,
    57, 112
Wood, James 51, 90, 98
    The Broken Estate 87 n.1
    "The Digressionist" 91
    How Fiction Works 87, 92
    The Irresponsible Self 87–93
Wood, Michael 22, 23
Woolf, Virginia 129, 135
Wordsworth, William
    The Prelude 135

Yeats, William Butler 45

Zeigler, Heide 32